THE WALL BETWEEN US

The Wall Between Us

A PROTESTANT-CATHOLIC DIALOGUE

by
BETTY KING

and
LORRAINE JULIANA

with a foreword by DALE FRANCIS

THE BRUCE PUBLISHING COMPANY • Milwaukee

(For that portion of the work written by Mrs. Juliana.)

NIHIL OBSTAT:

JOHN F. MURPHY, S.T.D.
Censor librorum

IMPRIMATUR:

✠ WILLIAM E. COUSINS
Archbishop of Milwaukee
January 13, 1964

Library of Congress Catalog Card Number: 64–17331

FOREWORD

When Betty King and Lorraine Juliana decided to carry on a Protestant-Catholic religious dialogue through correspondence, they were excited about the prospect.

The book that has developed from their correspondence is an exciting one.

It is exciting because it is plain that not only Betty King and Lorraine Juliana were involved in this correspondence; involved, too, in a most important manner was the Holy Spirit.

When Betty King, a convinced Protestant, and Lorraine Juliana, a convinced Catholic, began writing, they spoke of the wall between them. When they finished more than a year of exchange of views, the wall still remained but both had discovered there were many little walls that had been torn down.

We are separated not only by the wall between us, which is formidable enough, but even more by many little walls, false façades that should not be between us at all.

The letters of Betty and Lorraine tore away those little walls that should never have been there at all. They did this through love and respect for one another, through trying to understand one another and through the Holy Spirit working within this climate of love and respect.

So much of the work for Christian unity is being done by theologians that we sometimes forget the theologians represent the work on an intellectual level that cannot include the ordinary Protestant and ordinary Catholic.

When Christian unity comes — and I do not doubt it will come — it must come not alone among the theologians but among the people. Betty and Lorraine have demonstrated how the way for Christian unity can be cleared by ordinary people with an extraordinary love of God and extraordinary charity for neighbor.

It cannot be done by ignoring differences. Certainly Betty and Lorraine did not do this. They came right to the point of their disagreements, they said exactly what was on their mind to say, they discussed irritations, things in the other's faith that seemed ridiculous.

They discovered that many of the disagreements were misunderstandings, that irritations were sometimes unjustified, that what seemed ridiculous in another's beliefs were not ridiculous at all when seen through the other's eyes.

This change — both Mrs. King and Mrs. Juliana are changed persons after the correspondence — came not through argumentation but through, I am certain, the Holy Spirit and the Holy Spirit was able to work within them because they offered each other both love and respect.

The wall between us remains, even after we have torn away the false walls built by misunderstanding. When Christian unity comes this last wall will be torn away, but this will not be done by men but by the Holy Spirit.

What we can do is tear away the false walls, we can speak to one another with respect, we can offer one another love, and when we do these things we can be certain the Holy Spirit will be able to work within us.

This Betty and Lorraine demonstrate in this exchange of letters.

And one day, when enough of us love one another, when enough of us respect one another, when enough of us tear away the false walls of misunderstanding, when enough of us incline our spirits toward the Holy Spirit, that big wall between us will come tumbling down.

DALE FRANCIS

ACKNOWLEDGMENTS

The authors wish to thank the following publishers for permission to use quotations in this book from copyrighted material:

Desclee Co., Inc., New York, for permission to quote from *The Spiritual Life* by A. Tanquerey.

E. P. Dutton & Co., Inc., New York, for permission to quote from *The Divine Comedy* of Dante Alighieri, tr. Carlyle-Okey-Wicksteed, the Temple Classics Edition.

The Newman Press, Westminster, Md., for permission to quote from *Dark Night of the Soul* by St. John of the Cross, tr. E. Allison Peers.

Radio Replies Press Society, St. Paul, Minn., for permission to quote from *Radio Replies* by Fathers Rumble and Carty.

Hawthorn Books, Inc., 70 Fifth Avenue, New York 11, for permission to quote from *The Grace of Guadalupe* by Frances Parkinson Keyes, Copyright, 1941, 1953, by Frances Parkinson Keyes; and for permission to quote from *The Book of Mary* by Henri Daniel-Rops, Copyright, 1960, by Hawthorn Books, Inc.

The Episcopalian, Philadelphia, Pa., for permission to quote from the article "With Martha and Mary" by Mary Morrison in the July, 1960, issue.

Oxford University Press, Inc., New York, for permission to quote from *Enthusiasm* by Ronald Knox.

Sheed & Ward Inc., New York, for permission to quote from *The Council, Reform and Reunion* by Hans Küng, Copyright Sheed & Ward Ltd. 1961, published in the U.S.A. by Sheed & Ward Inc., New York; and for permission to quote from *The Confessions of St. Augustine* in the translation of F. J. Sheed, Copyright 1943 Sheed & Ward Inc., New York.

P. J. Kenedy & Sons, New York, for permission to quote from *Burnt Out Incense* by Father Raymond, O.C.S.O.

The Seabury Press, New York, for permission to quote from *The Lambeth Conference 1958*.

The Macmillan Company, New York, for permission to quote from *Mere Christianity* by C. S. Lewis, Copyright 1955.

Oxford University Press, London, for permission to reproduce the sonnet "In honour of St. Alphonsus Rodriguez, Laybrother of the Society of Jesus" by Gerard Manley Hopkins from the book, *The Poems of Gerard Manley Hopkins.*

The Confraternity of Christian Doctrine, Washington, D. C., for permission to quote from *The Revised Baltimore Catechism No. 2.*

Random House, Inc., for permission to quote from Charles Péguy's *God Speaks,* translated by Julian Green.

Harper & Row, Inc., for permission to quote from *The Choice Is Always Ours,* edited by Dorothy B. Phillips.

THE WALL BETWEEN US

Ethete, Wyoming
January 29

Lorraine Juliana
Carlsbad, New Mexico

Dear Lorraine Juliana,

A few weeks ago you asked your readers (in *Our Sunday Visitor*, "*Operation Understanding* Edition") to write to you. In so doing you threw out an idea which excited me. Ever since your column started appearing in *Operation Understanding*, I have enjoyed and appreciated it. Sometimes I have almost asked to have our name taken off the mailing list because a large part of the paper irritates me more than it conciliates me; but then I have thought, "No. I'd hate to miss Lorraine Juliana and the book and movie reviewers."

I am the wife of an Episcopal minister on an Indian reservation. Although the Episcopal Church bills itself as both Catholic and Protestant, I am personally unreconstructably Protestant. I'd like to write a book with you.

All kinds of books are coming out these days about the Catholic-Protestant Dialogue, but men are writing them. How would you like to try exchanging a series of letters with me for our own enlightenment and enjoyment, with a view to possible publication? What I have in mind is a Housewives' Dialogue between an unreconstructable Roman Catholic and an unreconstructable Protestant. I know you're busy; I am too. (Since starting this letter I have had a 20-minute chat with an old Indian woman who told me of the time when she took a long trip with another little girl on a travois; read 20 pages of a story about a lion cub to two preschoolers; thrown a load of clothes into the drier and another into the washer; drunk a cup of coffee; sampled a mystery thriller; buckled a two-year-old's shoes; and given out a handful of cookies.)

I have been writing a monthly column, somewhat similar to yours, in *The Wyoming Churchman.* Enclosed is what was supposed to be a valedictory column when the publication changed editorship and reduced the number of pages. I find that the new editors still want it but have supplied it with a new name, which they don't intend to tell me in advance of publication. I am wondering whether you chose "Striving for Sanctity" as the name for your column. Frankly it's the only thing I don't like about your approach. I think of sanctity as a by-product (somewhat like happiness), not something to strive for in itself. I believe that when we have fulfilled the commandment, "Thou shalt love the Lord thy God with the love of thy whole heart, and thy whole soul, and thy whole strength, and thy whole mind; and thy neighbor as thyself," then the sanctity is there of itself. (By the way, in quoting the New Testament I propose to use Ronald Knox's translation, which is the only one I have with an *imprimatur.* I am sorry that he chose to translate from the Vulgate rather than from the original Greek, but I'll let you know if I disagree with his translation. That's the Protestant in me!) When I started quoting these two Great Commandments, as we call them, I assumed they were a part of your Communion service, as they are of ours. (Much of the Anglican service, of course, has the same words in English as the Roman Catholic does in Latin.) Having checked into the missal which I asked for and received for Christmas, I see that they aren't in your Communion service; however, I am sure they are familiar to you.

I'd better stop now until I find out whether you are interested in carrying on a dialogue with me. My strongest resistance to your Church is that I feel it denies full personal freedom to the individual, and I believe personal freedom is one of the great gifts of God. So let me ask you this: if you want to enter a dialogue with me, will you feel that you must get clearance from your spiritual adviser? Will you feel that you want to talk the matter over with him even if you feel no obligation to do so? I have just looked up something in your missal. Would you be free to check into our *Book of Common Prayer?* If so, I'll be glad to send you a copy. (It contains our services of Morning and Evening Prayer, Holy

Communion, Baptism, etc., various prayers, the Psalter.) Conversion is not my aim. I respect your faith and your devotion.

How about it?

Sincerely,

BETTY KING
(Mrs. Ware G. King)

✝ ✝ ✝ ✝ ✝

J. M. J.

CARLSBAD, NEW MEXICO
February 4

Mrs. Betty King
Ethete, Wyoming

Dear Betty,

You used the right word: the idea excites me too!

A number of things in your letter intrigued me and started trains of thought that will be stimulating to pursue. The first was your thrice-repeated use of the word "unreconstructable" to describe not only yourself but me as well ("an unreconstructable Roman Catholic"). It's a matter of semantics, I know, and not too important, but because the word is not in my vocabulary and because the exact meaning, if not the connotation, eluded me, I headed for the dictionary (*Webster's Collegiate*, 1941, a relic of college days). The word wasn't there, so I looked up *reconstructed*—"made again, made anew; rebuilt." Taking it from there, I should imagine an "unreconstructable Protestant" could be assumed to mean one whose forebears had broken away from the authority of Rome so completely that even the thought of going back seems as ridiculous as trying to put Humpty Dumpty together again.

However, if that approaches the meaning of the word, I can't see quite how it can also be applied to a Catholic. So I expect the word itself is one of those words which, through usage, becomes familiar to a certain group and acquires connotations which are not readily grasped by those outside, and probably signifies about the same as "dyed-in-the-wool." There are many such words in Catholic terminology which mean little — or something entirely different — to those outside the Church. I remember when I first began reading Catholic literature eleven years ago (I am a convert, not a "born Catholic," as you probably know), I puzzled over many such words and often had to stop and consciously "translate" them before I could understand and go on.

Other things that demand thinking out and answering are, of course, the questions you posed about the title of my column and its implications, and the degree of personal freedom permitted in the Catholic Church, with the particular application in this instance being whether or not I would feel it necessary to get clearance from my spiritual adviser before entering a dialogue with you.

Let's take up the latter point first. As far as our exchanging a series of letters for our own enlightenment and enjoyment is concerned, there would of course be no obligation to seek permission from my spiritual director — although I probably *will* discuss it with him, because we are friends as well as confessor and penitent, and I know he will be interested.

The intention of eventually publishing the letters adds another dimension, however. I do not think I would need any official or unofficial "clearance" to write the letters, but they certainly could not be published — nor would I want them to be — without being submitted to the proper authorities to insure that there was nothing theologically unsound in them. Canon law requires this of "all writings which contain anything that particularly concerns religion and morals," and far from feeling this a denial of personal freedom, I think it a very wise and prudent safeguard, both from the aspect of assuring me that whatever I read carrying the *imprimatur* contains nothing dangerous to my faith (just as the Food and Drug Administration investigates and marks as safe only those products harmless to the body) and from the standpoint of protecting me from ignorantly or willfully publishing something that might do others spiritual harm.

I became a Catholic in 1951 because I became absolutely convinced that Jesus Christ had founded a Church, animated and guided by the Holy Spirit and hence indefectible, infallible, and indestructible, and that that Church is the Catholic Church. (Or Roman Catholic, if you prefer. I'm sure you are aware that Catholics themselves don't generally use the word "Roman." It is used mainly by non-Catholics to imply that the Church headed by the Bishop of Rome is only one among many presumably equally valid branches of the Universal Church, or to impute to it a foreign taint which is intended to make it suspect to other nationalities.)

I feel not the slightest loss of personal freedom in the Catholic Church; quite the contrary. Conversion, to me, was like finding a broad, well-paved, well-lighted highway with clear guideposts and warning signs erected at every dangerous curve and side road and precipice; after the "freedom" of being able to wander all over the mountainside in the dark, it was wonderful. I love being a Catholic — I would rather never have been born at all than have missed it, and if I tried a hundred years I could never put into words the overwhelming gratitude that floods me when I think how good God was to give me the gift of faith, which so very many people in the world, perhaps much more deserving than I, have somehow not received.

Do you feel it is a surrender of personal freedom to submit what you write to anyone else for approval? Does your husband read your columns before you send them in? Does he agree with all you write? Does the editor of the paper ever make any changes?

My column appears in three Catholic papers, all different: our diocesan edition of the *Register*, edited by a priest, which has carried it longest; *Operation Understanding*, with which you are familiar; and *The Wanderer*, a militantly conservative lay Catholic news organ. I mail the columns to all three editors simultaneously; no one here reads them first. Of the three, the priest is the only one who publishes the column every week without deleting anything. Dale Francis, editor of *Operation Understanding*, omits occasional columns, presumably because he prefers the space for something else, as he may later publish a column he didn't use when first sent in. *The Wanderer* does the same; the editor there also does not print columns (or omits certain paragraphs) which do not coincide with his political viewpoint.

I want to discuss the very interesting question you brought up about sanctity. Is it something to strive for in itself or a by-product? (Yes, the title of the column was my own idea.) But it's getting late and I think it would be better to let it go until next time. I hope you will tell me why you think God doesn't like "spiritual climbers."

To tie up other loose ends: Ronald Knox's New Testament is fine with me. I often quote from it myself, though sometimes I use the Confraternity of Christian Doctrine version, depending on which seems to express more clearly the particular point I'm getting at. I have a King James Bible too (from my Presbyterian Sunday School teacher for perfect attendance) which Father specifically told me *not* to get rid of when I entered the Church.

I imagine I will be able to refer to your *Book of Common Prayer* if you want to send it, as I have received permission on other occasions to read non-Catholic religious material. But I will ask permission, because obedience to authority is pleasing to God and because I could not logically expect His blessing to be with me in the reading if it were done in defiance of the laws His Church has made for my own spiritual safety and welfare.

Do you have a *Catholic Almanac?* I have two, neither current (1958 and 1959). Each contains some individual material (news events, papal speeches during the year, etc.) but also much basic handbook information regarding the Catholic Church that is the same in both books. I would be glad to send you one if you think you might find it helpful.

You have one advantage over me — you've read some of my columns, but I haven't seen any of yours except the one you enclosed (which I liked). I'd be happy to read any others you might care to send.

Pray for me — I for you.

Sincerely,
LORRAINE JULIANA
(Mrs. Joseph B. Juliana)

ETHETE, WYOMING

February 11

Dear Lorraine,

Hot dog. Let's go.

Your letter was most gratifying: first, because you didn't reject the Dialogue idea outright; second, because your response was stimulating and thought-provoking. "This gal has quality," thought I, and again, "Now I've met my match, or better than my match. Oh boy."

One of the immediate results of your letter was to send me scurrying around the house picking up socks and Tinkertoys, dusting the furniture, and vacuum cleaning the radiators, which have needed some drastic action for too long. I share with you an account of this unwonted activity because I get the impression from some of your columns that you share with me a disinclination toward housework. One of my best critics, an elderly farm woman who works harder than almost anybody I know, tells me that diligence in homemaking should spring naturally from love of the home folks; but I find that I can be a much better homemaker when I have something truly interesting to occupy my mind. Life with the family can go on from day to day, and I feel I can be fairly sloppy and still love them all and have their love, but I don't feel free to enter any exciting outside activity, like writing to you, when I am neglecting the household. Whenever I am scheduled to speak to a group, I feel a similar housekeeperly urge.

Next day, Monday

I am bone-weary tonight and find I cannot go on with any kind of intellectual discussion just now. I love God! I've always thought my Christian service should be largely verbal. I greatly enjoy leading adult Bible classes, counseling with people, talking to groups, writing about spiritual truths. So what have I been doing steadily for the past 16 hours until I am almost ready to drop? Feeding the hungry, clothing the naked, housing the homeless. A sudden thaw has left the record fall and winter snow nowhere to go but into the homes of about 10 families who live near the mission. Last night between 11 p.m. and 2 a.m. we settled 28 men, women, and children into the parish hall. At 4:30 a.m. another group, 16 individuals, arrived to be housed. By 5 we were busy preparing to cook breakfast for these 44 and 33 more who had been evacuated from their houses. As soon as breakfast was over, we started planning lunch; then dinner and another night. They are all tucked in now after countless efforts on the part of a great number of helpers; and I am bone-weary. I was awkward and less than efficient in transferring stew from one pot to another, pouring juice, and wrestling cots, but I thank God for the chance to be something other than verbal.

I'm sorry about the "unreconstructable." My use of the root word comes from Reconstruction days after the War Between the States. Quite a lot of people still call themselves "un-reconstructed Southerners." A more accurate way of saying what I was trying to say would be that, although I am now in a Church which calls itself both Catholic and Protestant, I personally have continued to be mostly Protestant in outlook. No, I don't think it would be right to use the word in reference to a Catholic, and my applying it to you was an inept way of saying "dyed-in-the-wool."

I must stop now if we are to meet a schedule. I am sending you all the "Dishpan" columns of which I have duplicate copies, along with a *Book of Common Prayer*. (I notice in the press that our Presiding Bishop presented one to Pope John awhile back, and the Pope promised to read it.) I should like to have a copy of the *Catholic Almanac*. Never heard of it before.

I'll pick up loose ends next week. The flood is subsiding now, and we should have lost our boarders by noon tomorrow at the latest.

I do pray for you. Tell me more about yourself so the prayers can be more intelligent. (I rolled over in bed Sunday morning and prayed first for my husband, whose Sundays are very full, and then for you. Instead of the "hold-up" prayer I had been using for you — just holding you in God's presence silently for awhile — I found myself praying for patience and calm as you got your family ready for Mass. When our children were very small, I came near losing my religion getting them ready to go to church. Was the prayer appropriate? I don't know how many children you have or their ages. We have Sarah, 11; Martha, 10; Ann, 7; and David, who will be 5 on Valentine's Day. In fact I feel about their ages as I do about the odometer in the car; everything is about to turn up one digit.)

Sincerely,

BETTY

✓ ✓ ✓ ✓ ✓

CARLSBAD, NEW MEXICO

February 23

Dear Betty,

I sat at the kitchen table after getting home from my hospital job the night your letter came, reading your columns and chuckling out loud. You've got it! — a funny bone, an apt way with words, a penetrating eye combined with great warmth — not to mention lots of faith, hope, and charity. Our dialogue is going to be fun.

Your March, 1960, column on being honest with God in our spiritual disciplines, on having to discipline yourself not to read but to work, found an echo here. A "disinclination toward housework" is putting it mildly. Like you, I am definitely not one of those women who are efficient and brisk in the parish kitchen. I stand around feeling lost and stupid and accept a dish towel gratefully when someone brighter hands me one. When the Altar Society has a bake sale I let the boys make a big batch of fudge (we have a dandy recipe), and when it's my turn to contribute to the Bingo refreshments I send a pound of coffee.

I liked April '60, about the choices ahead for your children in life and the fewer — and different sort of — choices still ahead of you. Almost in passing you mention, "Maybe I shall learn to play the piano, but I doubt it." Don't mark off the possibility! Mother gave us her old player piano last fall when we moved and I started taking lessons in December, at the age of 39, in the hope of learning enough to teach our kids, at least on the elementary level. Several for the price of one: it seemed a good investment. As a child I had taken lessons for a year from a neighbor but little of it stuck with me. I have a marvelous teacher now and am enjoying it immensely, though I can't say the same for my "pupils." They've found it takes patience and effort, and they're already losing interest.

We have seven children. Bob, the oldest, is 18, married, living 80 miles north of us, working days and taking college courses at night. Jerry is 15; Mike, almost 13; Mary, 7; Tony, 5; Jean, 4; and Betty, 2. (Incidentally, you have one of my favorite names. Jerry was "Betty" until he put in an appearance. When we finally did have a girl we named her Mary Elizabeth and I called her Betty, but Joe called her Mary, and after a few weeks I gave in and compromised with Mary Elizabeth. When I started *calling* her instead of just talking about her, the Elizabeth dropped off. But I finally got my Betty, and that is her name — Betty Marie.

If there were a scorekeeper in this game we're playing I'd concede a point. In my letter I commented that I love being a Catholic; in your reply you say simply, "I love God!" Me too. But there was a time when the very thought of becoming a Catholic was repugnant to me. I entered the Church because I became convinced beyond a doubt that it was the Church Christ established, divine and infallible; but the fact that I would *like* being a Catholic was a joyful surprise — a bonus, as it were.

Something you said suggests that you weren't always an Episcopalian. I'm interested in learning why you are one now, and what you mean by the statement that you are more Protestant than Catholic.

I liked what you said in your letter and in one of your columns about your "hold-up" prayer. Is it original? Do keep on praying for me: two Sundays ago Mass preparations went very smoothly, if I remember correctly. But did you forget me last week? Wow! I used your hold-up prayer as the subject for a column — hope you don't mind.

Your remark in a column about "spiritual climbers" being abominable in the sight of the Lord is still incomprehensible to me. It's just about the only thing in any of your columns that I couldn't say *Amen* to, myself.

I think — and it is traditional Catholic teaching, backed up by all the doctors and spiritual writers and mystical theologians that I have read — that if we're not climbing, spiritually, we're regressing. If we are not constantly trying to become better we are in serious danger of becoming much worse, because human nature is prone to take the line of least resistance; and the attractive temptations of the world, the weakness of our own flesh, and the machinations of the devil (do you share my appreciation for the *Screwtape Letters*, by the way?) will combine to drag us down from whatever level we may have managed, with the grace of God and our own efforts, to achieve.

So, since we have to climb or perish, why set our goals anywhere lower than the summit? It isn't enough to decide we'll be "good Christians" and let it go at that. Is a "good Christian" one who goes to church on Sunday and compromises all the rest of the week? There are times in every Christian's life when it takes heroic courage *not* to compromise — and will we have that courage if we are not trying constantly to become *more* like the Master? Jesus Himself tells us to be perfect (Mt 5:48) — and St. Paul says "What God asks of you is that you should sanctify yourselves" (1 Thes 4:3; Knox tr.) — or even more simply, in both the King James and Confraternity versions: "This is the will of God: your sanctification."

Adolf Tanquerey, whose *The Spiritual Life* is used as a textbook in seminaries, says the principal motives that may draw the faithful on to perfection can be reduced to three: (1) the welfare of our soul; (2) the glory of God; and (3) the edification of our neighbor. I could quote at great length from him to support my thesis. For instance: "In order to make sure that we shall not offend God grievously, the best means is to keep at a safe distance from evil by doing more than is strictly commanded and by striving to advance toward perfection; for the more we strive, with due prudence and humility, the surer we are of our eternal salvation." . . . "A perfect man gives more glory to God than a thousand ordinary souls" . . . "There is no better way to do good to others, to bring to God sinners or unbelievers and to strengthen the wavering, than the earnest effort to live a thoroughly Christian life. Just as a commonplace life on the part of Christians invites the critical and the unbelieving to scoff at Christianity, so true sanctity calls forth their admiration for a religion that produces such effects: 'By their fruits you shall know them.'". . . "Without the oft-renewed desire for perfection, there is no progress in the spiritual life."*

St. Teresa of Avila, famous mystic and the only woman classified among the Doctors of the Church, wrote in her *Life:* "Let us firmly believe that with the divine help and our own efforts we, too, can in the course of time obtain what so many saints, aided by God, finally attained. Had they never conceived such desires . . . they would never have risen so high. . . . Oh! how important it is in the spiritual life to rouse oneself to great things!"**

But I wonder — do the opinions of recognized Catholic authorities on the spiritual life carry any weight with you? In your eyes I suppose they are not authorities at all.

Thanks for the prayer book. I'll send an *Almanac* when I get hold of a book-mailer. Am enclosing a couple of clippings — the article about me appeared in our diocesan paper last summer†

* A. Tanquerey, *The Spiritual Life* (Tournai: Descleé, 1923), pp. 180–182, 207.

** Cited by Tanquerey, *op. cit.*, p. 207.

† Biographical data given in the interview: I was born in Lamar, Colorado, September 21, 1922. Because my father was a construction engineer with the state highway department we moved about frequently until I was six, when we moved to Roswell, New Mexico, and stayed. I was graduated from Roswell High School in 1940 and attended New Mexico A & M (now State University) on a tuition scholarship, working in an office half days to pay for my room and board. Majoring in English, I was on the staff of the college paper and was also active in the dramatics club and sang in a girls' quartet. In my sophomore year I married a fellow student, Joseph B. Juliana, of Gallup, New Mexico.

— and I ran across the Knights of Columbus ad last week in a magazine and it fit so perfectly with what I was intending to write that I clipped it out.

God love you. I'll be eagerly awaiting your reply.

Sincerely,

LORRAINE

✓ ✓ ✓ ✓ ✓

ETHETE, WYOMING

February 28

Dear Lorraine,

Brace yourself for a long one this time. Because of the flood and my weariness I skimped on my last letter and didn't begin to answer most of your first letter; so now I'll try to answer both your letters at once. Also, my husband is out of town for five days, and I have more time to write with fewer interruptions. I

During the war we lived for a year near Richmond, California, where my husband worked for the Kaiser shipyards; then I returned home to Roswell while he spent 2½ years in the Navy, the latter part on an aircraft carrier in the South Pacific. Our first son, Bob, was born in Roswell in October, 1943. Through the school year of 1944–1945 I worked as secretary to the principal of Roswell High School, my mother taking care of the baby, and I spent the next three years as secretary-receptionist for a Roswell surgeon, Dr. R. P. Waggoner. After his release from service, Joe worked for Safeway in Roswell for awhile and our second son was born there; then he came to Carlsbad to work in the potash refinery. We've been here ever since.

I had grown up in the Presbyterian Church, attended Sunday School regularly, sang in the choir, and was active in the Christian Endeavor (young people's society). At college I seldom went to church, though soon after our marriage both Joe and I had our membership letters transferred to a Methodist Church, on his employer's urging. We did not attend any church the first few years in Carlsbad. Then in 1951 I surprised my family by becoming a Catholic. For a while before this I had attended the Church of Christ, to which my sister and brother-in-law belonged.

From the time I could read, I wanted to be a writer. In the years between college and conversion I wrote a novel (unpublished) and acquired enough rejection slips from the slicks to paper a room. For six years after becoming a Catholic I didn't write at all. Since 1957 I have had articles and poems published in a number of Catholic magazines, and I have been writing the weekly column "Striving for Sanctity" since early 1959.

like having him around a lot in the daytime, but I also enjoy being a bit more to myself when he has to be away.

First I see that we shall have to tackle the "spiritual climbers" bit. What I said was about climbing, not climbers. Let me quote: "I have come, through the years, to see that spiritual climbing must be even more abominable in the sight of the Lord than social climbing. . . ." I make the distinction because I do not think of any person as being abominable in the sight of the Lord.

My *Webster's New International* (Second Edition; from what the reviewers say, I don't think I'll invest in the Third unless it comes out in paperback) says a "climber (*colloq.*)" is "One who by more or less unworthy means seeks admittance to a class superior, esp. socially, to his own." Spiritual climbing, in such a context, is a far, far thing from the striving for sanctity that you recommend so earnestly and persuasively. Mistake me not: I am for perfection and very much against the spiritual mediocrity that so perniciously pervades the aspirations of many church people these days. (I used to teach an adult Bible class of fine middle-classed people, and I was alarmed to discover that almost every one of them aspired to be "pretty good," and definitely no more than that. They didn't even want to be roused to want more: being better than "pretty good" might make them odd.) Spiritual climbing, in the derogatory sense I gave the expression, includes taking one's own spiritual pulse too frequently, looking around (and down) too often to see where one is in relation to other people, considering oneself to have "arrived," spiritually. It is, in essence, letting pride enter into the quest. In Canto IX of the *Purgatorio* the angel carves on Dante's brow seven P's, symbol of the seven deadly sins (*peccata*). Then in Canto XI comes what my literature professor designated "a definition of pride": "the great desire of excelling. . . ." Dante begins to find humility, and in the next canto an angel comes and brushes Dante's forehead with his wings, erasing the first P, Pride.

> While we were turning there our persons, "*Beati pauperes spiritu*" voices so sweetly sang, that no speech would tell it. . . .
> Now were we mounting up by the sacred steps, and meseemed I was exceeding lighter, than meseemed before on the flat;

wherefore I: "Master, say, what heavy thing has been lifted from me, that scarce any toil is perceived by me in journeying?"

He answered: "When the P's which have remained still nearly extinguished on thy face, shall, like the one, be wholly rased out,

"thy feet shall be so vanquished by good will, that not only will they feel it no toil, but it shall be a delight to them to be urged upward."*

If you, Lorraine Juliana, think I have Dante thus at my fingertips, think again. I don't, though I'd like to. Fact is, I was looking in a commentary for some further light on "Blessed are the poor in spirit," and I found a reference to the incident in Canto XII. I feel that I am just beginning, after years of perplexity, to understand what being "poor in spirit" means. I am not very articulate about it. (I have a feeling that time and time again I am going to annoy your lovely lucid logical mind by saying fuzzy things that have a meaning for me but not necessarily for anybody else. Keep hammering at me to be clear and you'll be performing a service, not only for thee and me, but also for some other people whom I don't really want to mystify.)

In my first letter I took issue with your column name, "Striving for Sanctity," and said I think of sanctity as a by-product. Your column which appeared February 18 in *Operation Understanding* was, in my opinion, a marvelous discussion of sainthood — up to the point that the gate came clashing down between us. You started with the definition of a saint as "a person who loves God with his whole heart and soul and mind and strength, and his neighbor as himself." Amen, say I. You went on to describe that love of God and its ensuing union; the soul's purgation of its attachments to sin; the seeing and serving of Christ in all one's fellow men; and the proper bearing of one's crosses. Amen, say I.

Then Clang! goes the gate. You go on to say, "The only human being who never sinned was Mary, the Mother of Jesus," and later in the column you talk about miracles that take place after the death of a saint, as a result of his or her intercession having been invoked. You believe these things; I don't. Your

* Dante Alighieri, *The Divine Comedy*, the Carlyle-Okey-Wicksteed translation (New York: E. P. Dutton & Co., Inc., the Temple Classics Edition).

willing, joyful submission to Mother Church leads you to believe them. This willing, joyful submission to the authority of the Roman Catholic Church is something that I must respect in you; but I believe it will constitute the chief and perhaps the only barrier between us.

I didn't tell my husband about my writing to you until I had received your reply indicating that you were willing to enter a dialogue. Then I showed him both our letters. He was interested but rather skeptical of the whole idea. "I always make it a point," he said, "not to enter into discussions with people whose presuppositions are different from mine." He thought we would come up against a stone wall from the very beginning.

I think we'll be in a bad way if we don't recognize that the wall exists; but I think further that we can accomplish a lot of good by smiling at each other over the wall, praying for each other to the God who is above the wall, and poking around its boundaries to find out where we really are in relation to each other.

I have a bit of a question about the publication of our dialogue, if it turns out to be publishable. You'd submit the letters to the "proper authorities" to insure that there was nothing theologically unsound in them. Now obviously an awful lot of what I write is going to be heresy from your standpoint. Will the authorities clear the whole lot if you will just give the "theologically sound" answers to my objections? I think they should welcome an encounter of this sort, for I am likely to be presenting the standard objections of a well-informed, unbigoted Protestant, and your answers could be helpful to a great many Protestants who are asking the same kind of questions. I'm just curious about whether your authorities would let my tainted apples into the barrel along with your pure ones.

I don't mean to tease you. If I get too flippant or hurt your feelings, you must let me know. I felt a very plaintive note toward the end of your last letter (I guess I should say your latter letter, but I do feel we've been corresponding longer than we have), when you wondered whether the opinions of recognized Catholic authorities on the spiritual life could carry any weight with me. I'll give you an answer which amused me very much when I heard it as coming from an American Indian who is a Catholic: "I go along with the Catholic Church in everything that doesn't conflict with my personal experience of God." The statement amused me because it is so un-Catholic and so typically Indian. (The Roman Catholics and the Episcopalians have a nearly clear field between them on this reservation, with just a bit of competition from Mormons, Jehovah's Witnesses, and a Pentecostal sect. I imagine the Opposition Priests have a frustrating time dealing with the very strong Indian sense of independence and resistance to authority that we find all around us.) Well, as for me, I accept as authoritative any statement on the spiritual life that rings true to my personal experience, but not just my personal experience. I want my personal experience to be backed up by as wide as possible a knowledge and understanding of history, literature, and life, and to be steeped in the Bible and the acknowledged Christian classics of the centuries (most of which, I'll freely admit, are Catholic). In other words I'm not campaigning for a strictly personal, subjective evaluation. I want correction and discipline, the sort of signposts you find in your Church. I can't accept your Church's set of signposts because I don't agree with you that your Church is indefectible or infallible. You've found a broad, well-paved, well-lighted highway and I grope along a narrow path, but I'm not wandering all over the mountainside in the dark. I have a Light. I find my correction and discipline from the indwelling Spirit of God; from other, more experienced travelers along the Way, both in person and in their writings; and to a certain extent from my Church.

Having begun, in the sentences above, to explain what I mean by the statement that I am more Protestant than Catholic, I shall go on with a bit of autobiography. (I very much appreciated the interview clipping you sent that told something of your life.) I was born April 11, 1925, in Winston-Salem, N. C., and grew up there as the youngest of five children. My father was manager of the credit department of a bank and a very faithful member of the Presbyterian Church, U. S. (Southern Presbyterian). I grew up nurtured by that church and owe a great debt to it. I was graduated from the R. J. Reynolds High School in 1942, the year my husband was graduated from The Protestant Episcopal Theological Seminary in Virginia. (We hadn't met.) After earning money for a while as special feature writer and news reporter for the *Winston-Salem Journal* I entered Agnes Scott College in the fall of 1943, going back to the newspaper job for the next two summers and also earning part of my college expenses in various Student Aid jobs on the campus at Decatur, Ga. Agnes Scott College is related to the Presbyterian Church. There I found my faith deepened, broadened, and enriched by the other students, the faculty members, and the works I studied. I majored in both English and Greek. Between junior and senior years, I spent six weeks in New York studying Christian ethics at Union Seminary (under Reinhold Niebuhr) and anthropology and philology at Columbia University. I planned to be a foreign missionary and had been working toward that goal for about six years. The first week I was in New York, I met Ware, who had also just arrived after spending four years in the Episcopal ministry in Idaho mining towns and was intent on some postgraduate study at Union Seminary and Teachers College. We very soon became intent on each other and were engaged early in the six weeks. I went back to Georgia to finish college, and he stayed in New York. We were married the following June, 12 days after my graduation. During my senior year I was teaching Sunday School to high school girls in the Presbyterian Church, attending weekly Quaker meetings on campus, and going to confirmation classes in the Episcopal Church. The combination may sound confusing, but I found it satisfying.

We spent the following five years in New York while he continued his studies and then served as assistant in a city parish; the next three in Trenton, N. J., where Ware served three churches at once; the following five in Riverton, Wyo., where he was rector of the one Episcopal church; and the time from September, 1960, until now here in Ethete (*Ee'*-thi-tih) with the Indians. The name of our church here is Our Father's House; *Ethete* is the Arapaho word for "good."

A story "by strangers quickly told," indeed, but as you know, a great deal was going on inside this outer shell of events all this time. It has taken me a long, long time to grow up, and I'm still a long, long way from the "real maturity" that St. Paul talks about in his letter to the Ephesians, that "perfect manhood, that maturity which is proportioned to the completed growth of Christ . . ." (Eph 4:13, Knox). But don't worry: I am *for* wholeness, holiness, perfection, sanctity. I hunger for them, and I rest not when I am not resting in Him.

I'm afraid all this is too much for one letter, although I meant to say a good deal more. Oh! One more thing. The name "hold-up" prayer is probably original with me, but the idea isn't. I got it from a saint named Nelle Morton who is now teaching Christian education in a Methodist seminary but who was influential in my Presbyterian youth as a Presbyterian herself. I believe Nelle may have taken the idea from Frank Laubach, the literacy man who is a genuine Protestant mystic. My sister Pat, who is married to a faculty member at that Methodist seminary, has her master's degree in English Bible from a Presbyterian institution but writes Methodist study material. There's a lot of cross-pollination among the Protestant denominations, as you may have gathered.

God bless you.

With love,

BETTY

✝ ✝ ✝ ✝ ✝

CARLSBAD, NEW MEXICO

March 11

Dear Betty,

Your most recent epistle was a joy to read. I will confess now to having been just a fraction disappointed in your second letter: you backed down so meekly on the "unreconstructable" and avoided the "spiritual climbers." I'm glad you clarified your stand on the latter. Your point is well taken: it isn't the climbing itself that is bad but the taking of one's own spiritual pulse and the looking down and around.

Have you ever read St. John of the Cross's *Dark Night of the Soul?* Doubleday has it out in an Image pocket edition. You'd like his discussion of the spiritual imperfections of beginners. He takes each of the seven capital sins in turn and indicates the imperfections common under each heading. Pride is first: I'll quote some of the key sentences:

"As these beginners feel themselves to be very fervent and diligent in spiritual things . . . they come to have some degree of satisfaction with their works and with themselves. And hence there comes to them likewise a certain desire . . . to speak of spiritual things in the presence of others, and sometimes even to teach such things rather than to learn them. They condemn others in their heart . . . resembling the Pharisee. . . . When confessors and superiors do not approve of their spirit and behavior . . . they consider that they do not understand them, or that . . . their confessors themselves are not spiritual. . . . Sometimes they are anxious that others shall realize how spiritual and devout they are. . . . Some of these beginners, too, make little of their faults and at other times become over-sad when they see themselves fall into them, thinking themselves to have been saints already; and thus they become angry and impatient with themselves, which is another imperfection. Often they beseech God, with great yearnings, that He will take from them their imperfections and faults, but they do this that they may find themselves at peace, and may not be troubled by them, rather than for God's sake; not realizing that, if He should take their imperfections from them, they would probably become prouder and more presumptuous still. . . ."* (As his contemporary mystic, St. Teresa of Avila, remarks of such souls in *The Interior Castle,*

---

* St. John of the Cross, *Dark Night of the Soul,* E. Allison Peers tr. (New York: Doubleday Image, 1959), pp. 39–42. Used by permission of the Newman Press.

"God grant that I have passed beyond this state myself; often I think that I have not!"*)

St. John of the Cross goes on to discuss the imperfections of beginners with regard to each of the other sins, not to discourage them but "in order that, realizing the weakness of the state wherein they are, they may take courage and may desire that God will bring them into this night wherein the soul is strengthened and confirmed in the virtues and made ready for the inestimable delights of the love of God."**

Don't worry about hurting my feelings or making me mad. Say what you think, frankly. I don't expect our censors will worry about your apples being in the barrel as long as it is quite clear which are the Catholic ones. I have shown our letters to two priests — my confessor and the editor of *The Southwest Catholic Register* — and both are very much in favor of the project and feel much good can come from it.

Actually, though, I am afraid I may be the one to irritate you. The Catholic's firm conviction that his Church is absolutely right and that therefore every other religion or exposition of religious beliefs is false, erring, or incomplete insofar as it contradicts, twists, or ignores basic Catholic dogmas, is bound to be galling to non-Catholics. From the outside the Church appears monolithic, authoritarian, totalitarian, intolerant, dogmatic.

From "inside" one has an entirely different concept of the Catholic Church. When we say "Catholic Church" we have in mind the true Kingdom of Christ on earth, a visible society founded by Christ; guaranteed by Him to last all days until the end of the world; commissioned by Him to teach all nations with His own authority; supernaturally guided and inspired and kept from doctrinal error by the Third Person of the Blessed Trinity; and governed to the end of time by the lawful successors of St. Peter, upon whom Christ bestowed the keys to the Kingdom and conferred the power of binding and loosing.

We see it, also, in a mystical but very real sense, as the Body

---

* St. Teresa of Avila, *The Interior Castle* (London: Sands & Co., 1946), p. 44.

** *Op. cit.*, p. 37.

of Christ: the living extension of her Divine Head, perpetually carrying on His work of salvation and sanctification in her members. As in a human body, the cells (the individual persons, the members) of the Mystical Body vary in function, in degree of viability, in usefulness. But because her Head is divine, because the Holy Spirit dwells within her, we submit to her authority joyfully, not blind to what is human and hence imperfect in her but venerating the infallibility and indefectibility with which God has vested her for our sake.

You speak of the wall that separates us and you put it very beautifully: ". . . we can accomplish a lot of good by smiling at each other over the wall, praying for each other to the God who is above the wall, and poking around its boundaries to find out where we really are in relation to each other."

But even that I see differently. To me, the only wall is that which individuals have built (and which their followers have shored up and extended and, sometimes, knocked out portions of) to try to limit the extension of the Kingdom of Christ into their lives. The various Protestant "reformers" built walls here and there; they said, "This we'll hang on to, but away with that!" And soon the lovely Kingdom was bordered with all sorts of walls and fences and hedges, and the Protesters built walls between themselves and each other, and those who came after them built more walls, and some of them kept moving farther and farther out — although they can all still see the King's castle over the walls and remain in touch with Him through the cracks and roads they left open.

Catholics build walls, too, of course, when they judge the teachings of the Church by their subjective feelings rather than judging their feelings and experiences in the light of the timeless and infallible teachings of the Church. Thus, your Indian, or the Catholics who say, "I can't go along with the Church on birth control" or divorce or some other doctrine that conflicts with their personal desires.

I think I can illustrate by discussing the two examples you noted when you spoke of the gate that came clanging down between us at my mention of the sinlessness of the Blessed Virgin Mary and of the miracles worked through the intercession of saints. Both of these walls (or the extensions of the one wall) seem from my point of view — please forgive me for being blunt! — to have been founded on ignorance and/or malice by the Reformers and/or their successors, and to be sustained to the present by the same two factors.

Either the wall-builders were ignorant of the theology underlying the Catholic teachings concerning the Mother of Jesus or they were so bitterly anti-Catholic that they threw her out just because Catholics made so much of her.

And either they did not bother to investigate the proofs of specific miracles which the Church has accepted (you'd be surprised how hard Mother Church is to fool and what stringent tests a purported miracle has to pass before it is declared authentic), or they refused to accept the evidence that God does work such miracles, because of the implications involved: (a) miracles performed by the saints show that they are true messengers from God; (b) miracles give divine confirmation to true doctrine; (c) only in the Catholic Church do such miracles occur. Most theologians would define a miracle as "an extraordinary event beyond the powers and outside the scope of any created agency, and therefore produced by God Himself." Please understand that I am not speaking of answers to prayer, which manifest the benevolence of Divine Providence and come to all who ask with faith and a sincere intention, but of real miracles such as the instantaneous fusion of broken bones with restoration of missing portions, or the sudden restoration of perfect sight to eyes whose corneas are scarred beyond repair. That is the type of miracle the Church requires in beatifying or canonizing saints.

But lest I be misquoting you again or endeavoring to demolish walls which do not exist, let me take you at your word and "hammer at you to be clear." In your letter you say, "You believe these things; I don't."

OK — what do you or don't you believe regarding the Mother of Jesus? (Personally, when I was a Protestant I didn't think about her one way or another; she was ignored in any sermons or church literature that came my way. But you have had much more formal study in Protestant theology than I had and are a minister's wife to boot.) Do you believe she did commit sins? Do you believe she was not preserved from original sin at the moment of conception? You do believe in original sin? (If I correctly interpret the Articles of Faith in the back of your *Book of Common Prayer*, the Episcopal Church affirms the doctrine of original sin. But also, if I understand your position rightly, you do not consider your Church infallible and accept what she teaches with some personal reservations.)

I think Dale Francis made a very perceptive observation in *Operation Understanding* some time back when he remarked that to most Protestants Mary is a historical personage, somebody who lived 2000 years ago, whereas to Catholics she is a living, loving Mother in heaven who hears our prayers and helps us in countless ways. To put it even more succinctly, to Protestants, Mary WAS; to Catholics, Mary IS. He said something else in this connection, too: that the actual fact isn't that we have set Mary up too high but that Protestants put Christ too low.

I did not become intimately acquainted with Mary immediately on entering the Church. I accepted the Church's teachings regarding her without reservations, but also without any depth of understanding or appreciation. The actual "coming to know her" was a more gradual process.

Did you ever meditate on what a privilege God bestowed upon Mary, a lowly maiden, humble, submissive ("Be it done unto me according to Thy word"), chosen from all the other women God ever has created or will create to be the Mother of His divine Son? Mother of the King of kings, Lord of lords, only-begotten Son of the Eternal Father, Redeemer of all mankind? Chosen to carry God in her womb, to give God a body of flesh and blood, to nourish God at her breasts, to live under the same roof with Him for thirty years and call Him "Son" . . . to gather the words that fell from His lips and the prophecies of those to whom the Father chose to reveal His identity and store them carefully in her heart . . . to follow Him during His teaching ministry and see the miracles He worked (and even to request miracles of Him, herself, as she did at Cana) . . . to stand beneath His cross? She takes no honor to herself; her glory is bestowed upon her by God, who chose her and exalted her above every other woman: "Behold, from this day forward all generations will count me blessed; because he who is mighty, he whose name is holy, has wrought for me his wonders!" (Lk 1:48–49, Knox tr.) Her only concern is to glorify God ("My soul magnifies the Lord") by drawing us closer to her Son. She loves us because He loves us; and she will even come down from heaven and work miracles if it seems necessary or desirable, to recall our attention to what He wants of us and to save souls.

Which brings us back to the other point: the miracles. You don't believe in miracles worked after the death of a saint as a result of his or her intercession. Why not? You surely would not limit God's power by saying He could not work a miracle if He chose. You believe in the Bible, so you must believe that Christ worked miracles and that He promised that His followers would also work signs and wonders that they might be believed. Do you believe that the "age of miracles" ceased once the Christian religion was firmly established? How do you explain Lourdes and Fatima?

Too many questions? Forgive me. Maybe I'm not much of an expert at poking around the boundaries of walls. I'm more the type to go charging into them, in an effort to knock them down. Please don't get mad and stop writing.

God love you. I do, *mucho*.

LORRAINE

✝ ✝ ✝ ✝ ✝

ETHETE, WYOMING
March 19

Dear Lorraine,

This dialogue is one of the most stimulating things that have ever happened to me. It's making a better Christian of me: as my husband, who is becoming very much impressed with what we are doing, says, "You must be absolutely sincere." He was speaking to me thus because I think he realizes the tough thinking that I face as I try to interpret my Protestant Christianity to you. You know, he had his reservations about the whole thing at first. Now his problem is to keep quiet when he'd love to jump into the dialogue feet first with his own thoughts and interpretations. He is controlling himself admirably. He starts to say something after reading our exchanges, and then he shuts his mouth and then opens it again to say simply, "It's your baby."

You asked in your first letter whether he reads my columns before I send them to the editor. In the first two and a half years of "The Rectory Dishpan" I often sent them in without his seeing them first. The editor never changed them, but as I look back at them (very few of these early columns are among the ones I sent you; I haven't extra copies), I can see that many could have been improved by editing. For three years, beginning with January, 1959, Ware and I edited the paper. He usually read my columns before we sent them to the typesetter, and he often made helpful suggestions, not about the theology but about the form. I have a tendency to go off at tangents, and he held me to one theme. We gave up the editorship after the December, 1961, issue, and I find for the first time in three years that I now have time to read almost all I want and to write much more than I was able to write when hours and hours went into copyreading, proofreading, correspondence to develop news leads, correspondence to shepherd our local correspondents, and headline-writing. Now that a new editor has taken over, I still submit my columns to my husband first, not because he asks me to, but because I trust his editorial judgment. Yesterday I turned one over to him. He read it and said, "You have two columns here." As soon as he said it, I knew it was so. The thing didn't cohere in the middle. Now I must do a rewrite job on one of the two or else put them both in the file and develop a fresh idea. The new editor will probably print my columns as they arrive to him, but I must wait and see whether he will make any changes. He is a person whom I trust. Being an editor has made me very tolerant and also appreciative of other editors.

You mentioned using the "hold-up" prayer idea in one of your columns. Feel free to use anything of mine. I'm interested in the widest possible circulation of any usable thought I may have.

When, in my Letter Two, I exclaimed, "I love God!" I was reacting to His way of dealing with me that day. I went on to detail the kind of Christian service I most enjoy — the verbal kind — and to explain the service that had reduced me to such a fagged rag that I couldn't answer your letter intelligently — the service of feeding flood refugees. I'm going into all this retrospective detail because I want to ask you about an anecdote in the life of your current companion, St. Teresa of Avila. Mary Ellen Chase, in lecturing at my college about 17 years ago, related the story, and I don't know whether I remember it with any accuracy. I think she said St. Teresa was traveling somewhere on a donkey when they came to a low place — perhaps a stream — and the donkey dumped her off onto the ground or into the stream. At this time she seemed to hear a voice, "This is the way I treat my friends." She picked herself up, dusted herself off, and replied, "No wonder you have so few of them." Is this story, or anything like it, in your *Life* of St. Teresa? It strikes a sympathetic chord in me. I told you I had wanted to be a foreign missionary, but I neglected to tell you that in the days I was working toward that goal, the only "foreign" culture I specifically rejected was the American Indian. Indians bored me. So here we are, plopped down in the midst of not one but two Indian tribes. Needless to say, Indians don't bore me any more; and I love God for that! One of my big sisters used to accuse me of wanting to be a missionary so I wouldn't have to wash dishes: she'd heard that foreign missionaries usually have house servants so they can get on with their missionarying and not spend all their time hewing wood and drawing water. Now, in this missionary situation, I find myself doing more menial work than I've ever done before. No steady workers are available to help out in the house, and I must leave the house to make coffee and wash dishes in the parish hall, tasks that other women usually do in a non-Indian parish. For these new duties I praise God. I have no opportunity to teach in any formal situations here; I must be content with small acts of mercy, like showing someone how to use a dial telephone or driving a woman in labor to the hospital 17 miles away. Infinite patience, abounding tact must take the place of my erstwhile abounding vocabulary. Thanks be to God for this new dimension of life. He has a lot to teach me.

Now: what do or don't I believe about the Mother of Jesus? (Just to set the record straight, I've had very little formal study in Protestant theology, and contrary to most Protestants' thinking, being a minister's wife does not make one a theologian by osmosis. It's true that I planned for years to be a Protestant missionary, but the thinking of our Presbyterian mission board was that a candidate should get the broadest possible general education before beginning to specialize in religious studies at the graduate level. Never having reached the level of graduate study, I never specialized in theology or religion courses.) I believe that Mary was a devout person and a good mother. I have come to have increasing respect and admiration for her since I have had children of my own. My reading of the Bible indicates that she bore at least six other children besides Jesus (Mt 13:55). Jesus showed His love and care for her in commending her to the care of John at the time of His crucifixion; but He also showed His true feeling about ordinary kinship ties in an incident recorded in all three Synoptic Gospel accounts, which I shall record from Mark 3:31–35, King James Version:

> There came then his brethren and his mother, and, standing without, sent unto him, calling him. And the multitude sat about him, and they said unto him, Behold thy mother and thy brethren without seek for thee. And he answered them, saying, Who is my mother, or my brethren? And he looked round about on them which sat about him, and said, Behold my mother and my brethren! For whosoever shall do the will of God, the same is my brother, and my sister, and mother.

All the statements outside the Bible that your Church has built up around Mary are, in my opinion, fabrications. The idea of praying to her, or to any of the saints, is repugnant to me. Jesus taught us to pray to our Father. St. Paul tells us (1 Tm 2:5, Knox tr.): "there is only one God, and only one mediator between God and men, Jesus Christ, who is a man, like them, and gave himself as a ransom for them all." And St. John says (1 Jn 2:1, Knox tr.): ". . . if any of us does fall into sin, we have an advocate to plead our cause before the Father in the Just One, Jesus Christ." The prayers of the people of God in the Bible are addressed directly to God. I like to believe, when I am praising God, that I am joined by and joining "angels and archangels, and all the company of heaven"; but I don't ever pray to these others. Prayer to anyone but God — Father, Son, and Holy Spirit — smacks to me of idolatry.

How do I explain Lourdes and Fatima? I don't. How do you explain the Devils of Loudun? But then I suppose you're forbidden to read about *them*. Your Church builds walls around your mind which are as indefensible, in my thinking, as the Berlin Wall. I suppose you would defend the *Index of Prohibited Books* as you do the *imprimatur*, with the Pure Food and Drug Administration analogy. On the night before I received your first letter with that analogy in it, I took part in a discussion group considering Milton's *Areopagitica, a Speech for the Liberty of Unlicensed Printing*. (This is not a church-related group.) The consensus there was that the licensing of drugs and the inspection of foods are not discussible in the same context as the licensing or censoring of literature. The human mind must have free access to all manner of thoughts and ideas in order to be fully free to choose what is true and good and beautiful. Foods and medicines can readily be tested and banned if they are harmful to the body. For one group of human judges to say that certain ideas are harmful to the soul and therefore to prohibit the spread of those ideas is a limitation on the individual person's freedom which I will not accept. Such prohibition leads to the suppression of truth, and I believe that all truth is God's. What does your supposedly infallible Church have to say these days about having forced Galileo to take back his theory that the earth revolves around the sun? Does the Roman Catholic Church still hold to pre-Copernican theories of astronomy? Does it accept modern psychology with the light that it throws on hallucination and mass hysteria? If it will listen to psychology, it can find reasonable explanations for the outbreaks of demonic possession in the convent at Loudun and for the claims of miraculous visions at Lourdes and Fatima. As for healing miracles, Oral Roberts and Christian Scientists testify extravagantly that such events occur outside the Roman Catholic Church. Granted, the medical investigations at Lourdes are thorough and do not admit the cure of functional diseases as true miracles; granted, an impressive number of genuine cures of organic conditions has been recorded at Lourdes, and countless other pilgrims have received spiritual blessings if not cures through the experience of taking part in the life around the shrine. In denying the objective fact of appearances by the Blessed Virgin to faithful people (most of whom seem to be ignorant peasant children) I am not pooh-poohing the validity and significance of mystical visions for the individual who beholds them. I am saying that a Roman Catholic peasant child or adolescent in a state of religious exaltation is likely to see a lovely lady in white with blue trimmings, while a Hindu peasant in mystic trance is likely to see a dancing divinity with an abnormal number of arms.

I have brought up Galileo; you may well bring up Thomas More as an example of a Catholic ill-treated by Anglicans. If I bring up the lecherous popes of former centuries, you can bring up Henry VIII. But I am free to admit that my Church has been wrong on many occasions, and you are not allowed to believe that your Church can be fallible. Have you discovered our "Prayer for the Church" on page 37 of the *Prayer Book?* In it we admit the possibility of corruption, error, and being amiss: "O Gracious Father, we humbly beseech thee for thy holy Catholic Church; that thou wouldest be pleased to fill it with all truth, in all peace. Where it is corrupt, purify it; where it is in error, direct it; where in any thing it is amiss, reform it. Where it is right, establish it; where it is in want, provide for it; where it is divided, reunite it; for the sake of him who died and rose again, and ever liveth to make intercession for us, Jesus Christ, thy Son, our Lord. Amen." Nobody in my Church asks me to consider it infallible.

Are Bingo and the Altar Society Bake Sale to be construed as a part of your infallible, indestructible Church? Or is this Church of yours simply an ideal, hanging somewhere in the pre-Copernican sky? Do you admit to shortcomings in your local parish's operation? Do some people in your parish criticize your priest? Do some of the women in the Altar Society indicate that they think they're better than some of the women who don't take part in its activities? What I'm really asking is, at what level does the infallibility begin?

Your Church requires you to believe in the nonscriptural doctrines of the Immaculate Conception and the Assumption of Mary. Rumor has it that you will in the not too distant future be called upon to believe in her as Co-Redemptrix with Christ. The last-mentioned would be a logical step in the procession of Mary from the simple peasant girl, favored of God, whom we meet in the Bible, to the Goddess your Church seems intent on making her. As I see it, your Church has started down a path of error and is removing itself farther and farther from simple Christian truth based on Scripture. I don't believe God stopped revealing Himself with the completion of the New Testament. I believe in the ongoing work of the Holy Spirit, but not confined to one "monolithic, authoritarian, totalitarian, intolerant, dogmatic" institution. The Mary of your Church is not the Mary of the Bible; the saints of your Church are not the same as the saints we meet often in the letters of Paul. A saint is a saint because God finds him so, and I don't think God is concerned with "proving" anybody's sainthood so that somebody can be added to your calendar.

I must stop now. Thank you for the *Catholic Almanac*. It is proving helpful to my understanding and instructive to my use of terminology. I want to ask you about the place of English hymns in your Church. Are they used in any of your services? If not, when are they sung, and by whom? (By English I mean any hymns sung in the English language.) How authoritative is the Bible for you? Do you defend Latin as the sole liturgical language for the Church? If you would prefer the use of English in services, would you be free to say so?

I've been pretty rough this time. Let me assure you that although I deplore the walls your Church builds to keep its people in (for an added example, forbidding them to worship God in any other church), I greatly respect and admire some of the people your Church produces.

And I love you.

BETTY

✓ ✓ ✓ ✓ ✓

CARLSBAD, NEW MEXICO

March 27

Dear Betty,

Ouch! "Rough" is putting it mildly. You were brutal. It's going to take a lot of words and a lot of pages to answer all the questions and try to clear up all the problems raised by your last letter, but hold your breath: I'm going to try!

I was very much interested in what you told me of your husband's reaction to our dialogue. He sounds like a nice person, and I have no doubts regarding your sincerity. One thing I am finding intriguing, however, is the way each letter you write seems — in retrospect, at least! I'm not going to get them out and read them over now — to reveal a different aspect of your personality. The first letter was challenging — friendly, questioning, a little guarded. The second revealed a warm, tired, human, happy side. Number Three was written with a twinkle in your eye (the apples are what I remember in it). But something I said must have stung: in Number Four you took your gloves off and blasted out with both barrels of your shotgun. This analysis is for free — just a thought that struck me and I wanted to share.

Yep, the story about St. Teresa of Avila is true, as far as I know; I've read it repeatedly. She was quite a gal. Listen, if I send you some books from time to time, do you think you'd be interested in reading them? Every letter brings up something that makes me think, "Oh, how she'd enjoy such-and-such a book!"

Two things make me hesitate: one is the fact that I don't have duplicate copies of any of my books and harbor the (perhaps selfish) fear that I might want to look up something for a column in a book that wouldn't be here when I'd need it; and the other is doubt about how it would fit in with the purposes of our dialogue as far as possible future publication is concerned, to be reading things on the side instead of putting everything in our letters. And a third cause for hesitation, too: if you are as busy as I am you might not even want anything else to read. However, you did say you have more time for reading now, and I can no longer resist the temptation to send you *The Woman Shall Conquer*, a popular report of all our Lady's appearances in modern times. There is another book I would be more inclined to send if I still had it, but I loaned it to a girl who moved away without returning it: *The Immaculate Heart*, by John di Marchi (if I remember the spelling of his name correctly). It was a detailed record of the Fatima visions and subsequent events concerned with them, including verbatim records of all the interviews with the children, verbatim news stories, and personal observations of the "miracle of the sun," etc. — a much more scholarly and fully documented study than the Sharkey book, which is aimed primarily at Catholics and may not explain and "prove" everything to the satisfaction of a critical non-Catholic reader. But I shall be eager to hear your reaction to it and assure you that it is not fiction.

As far as Mary having borne other children besides Jesus is concerned, I am afraid that is a theory that is put forth by some primarily in order to differ from Catholic doctrine. That is, some of the early Reformers were so sure the Church of Rome was wrong in virtually everything she taught (the beast with the seven heads and ten horns, leading astray the inhabitants of the earth) that they spent a good part of their time attempting to prove it. They "searched Scripture" looking for texts to use against her. But there is nothing in Scripture, properly understood and interpreted, that can possibly contradict the doctrines officially taught by the Catholic Church, because both the Bible and the Church are given to men by God for their instruction and sanctification, and God cannot lie or contradict Himself. Although the Bible doesn't specifically state that Mary had no other children besides Jesus, the oral tradition of the Catholic Church maintains that she was a virgin before, during, and after the birth of Jesus — "Mary ever virgin." There were a few early Christian writers, Tertullian and the Arian Helvidius among others, who held that Mary had other children, but the vast majority of the Fathers held that such an opinion was blasphemous; and by the end of the fourth century her perpetual virginity was accepted doctrine in the Catholic Church.

In Matthew 13:55, the word "brethren" proves nothing: any relatives, even in the third or fourth degree, or members of the same tribe, were entitled brethren by the Jews. And in Matthew 27:56 reference is made to "Mary, the mother of James and Joseph" (two of the "brethren" of Christ, mentioned above), obviously not referring to the mother of Jesus. The fact that Jesus commended her into the keeping of John, the son of Zebedee, at His crucifixion shows that she had no other children of her own to care for her.

Mary's words to the angel, "How can that be, since I have no knowledge of man?" when she was already betrothed to Joseph, are generally held by Catholics to indicate that she had taken a vow of virginity. Joseph knew her Child was conceived by the Holy Spirit; to him, as to us, the mere thought of her becoming a mother to merely earthly children after bearing the Son of God Himself would have seemed a sacrilege. (And to take care of a couple of other objections which you didn't mention but Protestants frequently do bring up, the word "firstborn" does not necessarily imply that she had other children: it was a position important in Jewish tradition and law, and parents did not have to wait until they had other children before they could call their first child "firstborn." And the word "till" in Matthew 1:25 [King James trans.; Knox uses "when"] does not necessarily mean Joseph "knew" her afterward.)

I don't really know what you meant to prove by the quotation from Mark 3:31–35 — "Whosoever shall do the will of God, the same is my brother, and my sister, and my mother." Jesus was certainly not denying that Mary was His mother, nor was He being disrespectful to her: He was pointing out that far more important than any blood relationship was obedience to God's will. And can you name anyone more obedient to God's will than Mary? (And incidentally, the last sentence cannot possibly be literally true, so why must the words "brethren" and "sisters" be taken so literally in the previous passage quoted?)

All of the references you quote in the next paragraph, about Christ being the only mediator between God and man, are familiar to me and are accepted without reservation by all Catholics.

Then you say that prayer to anyone but God smacks to you of idolatry.

We do not idolize Mary or the saints: we honor them. The Catholic Church never has and never will "make Mary a goddess," as you charge later on in the letter. Your *Book of Common Prayer* has the Apostles' Creed (p. 15), and Article VIII states that the Creeds are to be thoroughly believed and received; so you presumably believe in the Communion of Saints. This doctrine is based on the fact that all Christians are members of the Body of Christ, the Church, and can help one another spiritually as well as physically (see 1 Cor 12) — and this includes the Christian saints who are already with Christ in heaven. There are numerous passages in the Bible indicating that we should pray for each other (see the beginning and end of St. Paul's letters: for example, 1 Thessalonians 5:25 and 2 Thessalonians 1:11). What is wrong, then, with asking the saints in heaven, who are in the very presence of God Himself, to pray for us, if we can ask those on earth to pray for us? There is only one Mediator, Christ; but why does St. Paul ask the Thessalonians to pray for him? — why doesn't he just pray to Christ for himself? He is asking them to intercede *with Christ* for him, and he tells them he prays always for them, thus acting as a mediator himself between Christ and them. It is scriptural that we may benefit by each other's prayers and that there is nothing wrong with asking another to pray for us. Catholics simply believe that such requests for prayers are not limited to persons still on earth but can logically and efficaciously be directed also to saints already enjoying the beatific vision of God in heaven. And does not the fact (it *is* a fact) that such prayers are often answered with astonishing promptitude and even with miracles indicate that it is God's will that we pray thus?

You can get to heaven without ever praying to a single saint. Their assistance is only intercessory: it is God from whom all graces and favors ultimately must come. But you might get many more graces if you acknowledged and thanked and glorified God for all those holy Christians who have lived before you, and if you asked them to pray for you. The Church has canonized thousands of holy Catholics, from every century in the nineteen and a half centuries since Christ, and there are myriads of uncanonized saints in heaven. In canonizing saints the Church sets them up for us to admire and try to imitate, just as we set up Washington and Lincoln as patriotic heroes (her only concern in "proving" their sanctity is to make certain she is not setting up a hero with clay feet) — and she urges us to honor the saints in heaven because they served the Lord Christ so faithfully on earth, and because in honoring them we are glorifying God who worked in them "both the will and the performance" (Phil 2:13; Conf. tr.). They can help us with their prayers and example now, and when we get to heaven one of our special joys will be in greeting all those wonderful friends of God who have inspired us by their example and assisted us by their intercession.

And, of course, heading them all is Mary. We do not honor Christ less because we give so much honor to His mother: rather, we love and honor her because we *worship* her divine Son who deigned to take His human nature from her, and because she, more than any other created being with free will, lived in perfect accord with God's will.

It was through Mary's intercession that Christ's first public miracle was performed, at Cana (Jn 2:1–11). She noticed that the wine was running out, and to save their hosts embarrassment she called it to her Son's attention. Despite what seems a not very encouraging reply, she has no doubt either of His ability or His willingness to come to the rescue; she tells the servants to

"Do what He tells you" and thus is undeniably responsible, to some extent at least, for His having worked the miracle at all. She does the same thing today. It is not that she tells Him anything He does not already know; it is simply that it is His will that sometimes our needs not be answered until she does intercede for us.

I am not familiar with the Devils of Loudun and have found no reference to them in any book I have. You may be right in saying I am forbidden to read about them, at least in the version you've read: if it is a book on the Index, I am. The books forbidden are those which attack the Catholic religion and the Catholic Church or are likely to undermine faith or morals. I find this reasonable and do not resent it. You say, "The human mind must have free access to all manner of thoughts and ideas in order to be fully free to choose what is true and good and beautiful." A man who has reason to doubt whether he has the truth or not should certainly try to find the truth. But Catholics know they have the Truth (though it is ever subject to better understanding and deeper development). Theologians and scholars and apologetes and the like can get permission to read books on the Index because it is presumed that they will be able to separate the false or inaccurate or misleading statements from those which correspond to the truths which God has revealed. But the ordinary Catholic can get terribly confused and upset by reading things which attack his faith, especially if the writers quote a lot of Scripture that seems to back up their arguments; he doesn't know his religion or his Bible well enough to discern the fallacies or to refute them. The Church forbids the reading of books by her subjects which will endanger their faith not because she fears the books might be right but because her less well-instructed members might fail to see where they are wrong. The Index needs periodic revision, because books which were dangerous at one age may be of only academic interest at another. But what goes into the mind is infinitely more important than what goes into the body, and I feel not the slightest resentment at having a wise and experienced spiritual Mother who marks certain books as off bounds because they are unhealthy spiritual food; I would think her remiss in her duty if she didn't.

Well, let's go on. You ask, "What does your supposedly infallible Church have to say these days about having forced Galileo to take back his theory that the earth revolves around the sun?"

You have the usual Protestant misunderstanding of the meaning of infallibility as claimed by the Catholic Church. The doctrine simply means that the Church is protected by the Holy Spirit from teaching error in matters of faith or morals. It does not mean that any individual or group of individuals in the Church cannot err, with the exception of the Pope when he is speaking in his official capacity as Christ's Vicar on earth, defining a doctrine which concerns faith or morals and is binding on all the faithful. In his other writings and utterances he can make mistakes; even encyclicals do not come under the definition of infallible, although good Catholics certainly respect and honor the opinions expressed therein.

The bishops of the Church, convened in an ecumenical council in union with the Pope, have a collective infallibility; even so, their definitions are not official until confirmed by the Pope.

The question of infallibility was not involved in Galileo's condemnation. I will quote from my reference book on this: "The Committee of Cardinals and theologians appointed by the Pope to inquire into the theories of Galileo gave the verdict that they were false and contrary to Holy Scripture and that Galileo himself was gravely suspect of heresy. After the decision was given the Pope sanctioned it. The decision, of course, was wrong. But the conditions required for infallibility were not present. . . . All who understand the conditions required for an infallible decision by the Catholic Church have long since given up the Galileo case as having any bearing on the question at all."*

Once an infallible decision has been made it stands for all time. It would be absolutely impossible for one Pope to define a given doctrine and for a subsequent Pope to define a contradictory doctrine.

---

* Rumble and Carty, *Radio Replies* (St. Paul, Minn., 1940), Vol. II, No. 396.

Infallibility does not mean "inspiration": it does not mean that the Holy Spirit tells the Pope what to say. Popes study and do research and consult with theologians and bishops; they do not wake up one morning, say, "Hm, that was some vision I had last night; guess I'd better define a new doctrine today." The doctrine of infallibility is better expressed negatively: it means that God will not permit the Pope to define ex *cathedra* a doctrine not in accordance with the genuine teaching of Christ. "*Ex cathedra*," of course, means that the Pope is speaking not as a private theologian but in view of his office as supreme head of the whole Church on earth, giving a decision for all the members of the Church on a matter of faith or morals.

Infallibility does not mean "impeccability." It does not mean that the Pope cannot sin, although the great majority of Popes have been men of above average virtue, particularly in recent times. No Catholic denies that there have been a few bad Popes. (One book I consulted says six or seven; this would be about one in forty, it points out, and in the Apostles chosen by Christ Himself the ratio was one in twelve.) The Pharisees were accused of numerous sins by Christ, for "they say, and do not" — yet He told the people they were still to be heeded, because "they sit in Moses' seat: All therefore whatsoever they bid you observe, that observe and do; but do not ye after their works: for they say, and do not" (Mt 23:2–3, King James). No bad Pope ever defined a wrong doctrine or pretended his own conduct was in accordance with Catholic moral principles. As a matter of fact, wouldn't the very existence of the bad Popes, considered in the light of the enduring stability of the Church through all the time since Pentecost, be an additional indication of the supernatural character of the Church, which cannot be destroyed by enemies without or bad weeds within?

Obviously, the Church does not still hold to pre-Copernican theories of astronomy. Equally obvious, such matters are outside the field to which infallibility is restricted. (Is it necessary to mention that Bingo and Altar Society bake sales have nothing to do with infallibility either? Or that the answer to Questions No. 3, No. 4, and No. 5 in that paragraph is Yes?)

In the paragraph just above that you mention Thomas More and Henry VIII and state, "I am free to admit that my Church has been wrong on many occasions, and you are not allowed to believe that your Church can be fallible." I am perfectly free to admit (as I have) that individuals and groups of Catholics can err or sin, whether they be in high places or low. You say nobody in your Church asks you to consider it infallible. But Christ Himself promised to send the Holy Spirit to keep His Church from error, to bring to mind *all* He had taught (John, Chapters 14 and 16) — of which not all was written in the Bible (Jn 21:25). If He established a Church, as Scripture indicates He did and as I believe you will admit, it was certainly within His power to insure that she would be a true and reliable teacher and guide. There is only one Church which claims that infallibility; how can anyone who really gives the matter serious thought prefer to belong to a Church which admits it may be mistaken in what it teaches?

I am afraid you are wrong in denying the objective fact of the visions at Lourdes and Fatima because "a Roman Catholic peasant child or adolescent in a state of religious exaltation is likely to see a lovely lady in white with blue trimmings." The exact opposite is true: the Blessed Virgin chose to appear (or God chose to send her) to ignorant, not particularly religious peasant children so there could be no doubt of the supernatural nature of the revelations. "Out of the mouths of babes . . ." Think of the children to whom she appeared: children who have no schooling at all or are slow at learning, who are unable to read at eleven or thirteen, who are scarcely capable of memorizing a simple prayer like the Our Father after long coaching — but remember every word the Lady says to them, giving identical versions when questioned separately and repeatedly by various interrogators over a long period of time, questioned too by unfriendly examiners who are trying to trip them up and make them admit they are lying and who resort to tricks and threats and even imprisonment to gain that end. Children who repeat what they saw and heard, literally and simply, without the glosses an adult might insert. Children who were not praying "in a state of religious exaltation" when the Lady appeared: Bernadette of Lourdes was taking off her shoes to wade an icy stream, the children of Fatima were gathering their sheep to start home because a flash of lightning had made them fear a storm was coming, the shepherds of La Salette had waked from a nap and were hurrying to gather their knapsacks and water the cows before driving them home for the night. In each case the authenticity of the message given by the Lady is proved by prophecies later fulfilled and by miracles. The "prodigy of the sun" at Fatima on October 13, 1917, was witnessed by some 80,000 to 100,000 people, including skeptics, atheists, and people in cities miles away who had no knowledge of anything going on at the Cova da Iria. The message at each apparition was substantially the same: "Do penance or you shall all likewise perish!"

Are you still with me? I'm down to the last page of your letter and there are still a few questions to answer. You ask about the use of English hymns in the Church. That is the one thing that I, as a convert from Protestantism, find lacking in the Catholic Church — the fellowship, the solidarity, the *communion* of singing together — praising God, thanking Him, telling Him of our weaknesses, and asking His help in song. St. Paul exhorted his converts to praise the Lord with psalms and hymns and spiritual songs, and it seems to me that non-Catholic Christians follow this advice more faithfully than the Catholic laity are currently in the custom of doing. (I specify *laity* because the situation is different in monasteries and convents.)

My own experience as a singing Catholic is limited to this one parish, which may not be entirely typical, but it appears that the average lay Catholic knows so few hymns that they can all be printed on the front and back of a sheet of cardboard — and he gets very little opportunity to sing even these. Perhaps two thirds of them are in English. The schoolchildren learn a few hymns, as does the choir, which they may sing during a high Mass, but the congregation does not join in the singing, and the ordinary Catholic attending services very seldom gets to sing anything but the *Tantum Ergo*, the *O Salutaris Hostia*, and *Holy God, We Praise Thy Name* at Benediction.

Every once in a while, since becoming a Catholic, I get out my old Church school hymnal and have myself a wonderful time singing all the old favorites with a joy and faith and understanding that goes much deeper than when I sang them as a Protestant. I find myself going around singing, "What a Friend we have in Jesus, all our sins and griefs to bear! What a privilege to carry everything to God in prayer!" and meaning every word of it from the bottom of my heart and rejoicing that it is so.

I sing: "Love Divine, all loves excelling, Joy of heaven, to earth come down: Fix in us Thy humble dwelling—" . . . and: "Spirit of God, descend upon my heart . . . And make me love Thee as I ought to love!"

I sing: "All hail the power of Jesus' name . . . And crown Him Lord of all!"

And: "Come Thou, Almighty King!" . . . "In the Cross of Christ I glory!" . . . "This is my Father's world—" . . . "Jesus calls us o'er the tumult of our life's wild restless sea . . . saying, 'Christian, follow Me!'" . . . and many, many more.

I think that is the only thing I really miss. We have so much that Protestants don't have and don't even know they lack: the essentials, the big things: the Eucharistic Presence in our tabernacles and in ourselves after every Holy Communion, the certitude of absolution in the confessional, the other Sacraments, our devotion to Mary and our wonderful familiarity with all the other saints, the multitude of helpful sacramentals, the rich theological treasury of the Fathers and doctors and holy writers of the Church, and so many other helps to holiness that non-Catholics lack entirely or have in less abundance. But you do have an edge on us in this tradition of hymn singing on the parish level. This is being recognized by many Catholics, particularly those who are converts. I am sure you are aware of the liturgical revival going on within the Church and the increasing tendency toward more active lay participation in the services. I am sure you can also see that this is a matter of custom rather than of doctrine and has no bearing on the question of infallibility. I am perfectly free to believe that singing hymns in English is good and free to sing hymns composed by Protestants unless they contain heretical statements, and, offhand, I can't think of any that do.

How authoritative is the Bible for me? I believe that the Bible is the inspired word of God, that it contains no error, that it is "useful for teaching, reproving, correcting," etc. It is on who is qualified to interpret the Bible that we disagree. Protestants believe in the principle of "private interpretation" — that the Holy Spirit will assist each sincere searcher for truth in discovering and applying the meaning of Holy Scripture. Catholics believe that "no prophecy in Scripture is the subject of private interpretation" (2 Pt 1:20) but that Christ founded a Church to teach all men, that He promised to be with it all days (Mt 28:20), to send the Holy Spirit "to dwell with you forever, the Spirit of Truth" . . . who "will teach you all things and bring to your mind whatever I have said to you" (John, Chapters 14 and 16 again).

We believe that the Bible belongs to the Church. The "books" of the New Testament — the four Gospel stories, the account of the Acts of the Apostles after the Resurrection, the epistles of St. Paul and of SS. Peter, James, John, and Jude to the various congregations, together with St. John's Revelation — were written by members of Christ's Church under the inspiration of the Holy Spirit for the instruction and edification of believers and unbelievers. These and a number of similar writings were treasured and copied and passed from one congregation to another. After several centuries all such writings were gathered and scrutinized carefully to determine their authenticity, and in the year 374 at the Council of Rome the Pope published the list (Canon) of inspired works of the Old and New Testaments.

Hence it was the Catholic Church, by virtue of the infallibility vested in her by the Holy Spirit, that determined which writings were inspired and which, though likewise claiming inspiration, were "apocryphal." Scripture is a divine aid committed by God to the living Church, and only the Church has the authority to say, infallibly, what is meant by any passage in Holy Scripture. You can read a passage and say, "It means *this*." I can read it and say, "No, it means *that*." But we can both be wrong. The Holy Spirit couldn't possibly be inspiring all the contradictory interpretations that are put forth today.

Christ commissioned the Church to teach all the world the truths revealed for men's salvation. Jesus did not write a word for posterity to read. There is no place in the Bible where we find Him telling His Apostles to write anything. There is no passage in the Bible stating that everything one needs to know for salvation is to be found in Scripture, your Article VI notwithstanding, or that one must not believe anything unless it is written there. In fact, St. John specifically states that Jesus did and said other things that were not written (Jn 21:25, quoted above). St. Paul wrote to the Thessalonians: "So then, brethren, stand firm and hold the teachings that you have learned, whether by word or by letter of ours" (2 Thes 2:15, Confraternity) — "Keep to the pattern of sound doctrine thou hast learned from my lips" (2 Tm 1:13, Knox tr.) — "Thou hast learned, from many who can witness to it, the doctrine which I hand down; give it into the keeping of men thou canst trust, men who will know how to teach it to others besides themselves" (2 Tm 2:2, Knox tr.). In other words, the Apostles were to pass on what they had learned *by word of mouth* to their legitimate successors. And this succession was passed down through "the laying on of hands" (see Acts 13:3; 1 Tm 4:14; 2 Tm 1:6) — and by the grace of God this succession has never been broken in the Catholic Church.

Individual Christians and even priests have departed from the truth and "turned aside to fables" in every century, many of them taking thousands of followers with them (here's where a study of the history of the Church is fascinating, with the many heresies — Arianism, Nestorianism, Manichaeanism, Albigensianism, Lutheranism, etc.) — but the Catholic Church has preserved the teachings of Christ without error. Through the centuries she has studied and taught and expounded and explained, coming gradually to a better understanding of many things which are only hinted at, perhaps, in the Bible (for example, the role of the Blessed Virgin Mary). She has never taught any new dogmas of faith but only *developed,* under the infallible guidance of the Holy Spirit, the deposit of truths revealed by God and placed in her charge.

Christ gave her (through Peter and his successors) the authority to discipline her subjects and to make rules and regulations for the spiritual welfare of her members: "Whatever thou shalt bind on earth shall be bound in heaven . . . (Mt 16:19, Knox tr.). Thus she can make disciplinary laws and change them when circumstances warrant (like the rule to abstain from meat on Friday, whose purpose is to keep reminding us that Christ died for us on Good Friday and also to help us "mortify our members" and do penance lest we perish).

Yes, Latin as the liturgical language of the Church is fine with me. I have a Latin-English missal (several of them, in fact) and can follow along easily. I have often attended early morning Mass at San Jose Mission here; we used to live closer to it than St. Edward's and the Mass schedule on weekdays was more convenient. It is a Spanish-speaking parish; sermons and announcements are in Spanish at some of the Sunday Masses and confessions are heard in Spanish or English. But the Mass is identical with that at St. Edward's. I follow it with my missal and the Spanish-American communicants follow it with their Latin-Spanish missals, and we are all worshiping together without the slightest feeling of strangeness, truly brothers in Christ. It would be the same if I were to go to a Catholic Church of the Latin rite anywhere in the world. The only change I would like to see made — and of course I feel free to say this — is in the reading of the Epistle and Gospel of the Mass. They are for the instruction of the congregation rather than directed to God, as is the rest of the Mass, and I think it would be much more practical to read them aloud in the language of the people for the benefit of those who are not using missals. On Sundays the Epistle and Gospel are repeated in the vernacular facing the congregation after being read first in Latin at the altar, but on weekdays the Mass is entirely in Latin without interruptions.

[Note: Since writing this the weight of the arguments in favor of having the entire Mass in the vernacular has won me over. See my last letter. L. J.]

We do not join in the public worship of God in other churches because we believe He has revealed to His Church the manner in which He wants to be worshiped and that, knowing this, it would be wrong to join in public worship with those who have departed from the divinely sanctioned mode of worship to forms of their own choosing. It would imply that one way was as good as another, and this we do not believe: only in the Catholic (and schismatic) Churches is God worshiped in the true Sacrifice of the Divine Victim upon the altar by a validly ordained priest. It is not that we do not believe in your personal sincerity in worshiping God your way, or that God does not accept your worship. We believe in your good faith and we can pray with you privately, but we cannot join with you in a public service because attendance would imply that one form of worship was as pleasing to God as another.

Whew! Are you as tired as I am? I've spent so much time on this letter that the housework and ironing and even my piano practicing(!) have been neglected; I'll be happy to get it in the mail.

Pray for me — I for you.

With much love,

LORRAINE

✝ ✝ ✝ ✝ ✝

ETHETE, WYOMING

April 8

Dear Lorraine,

Your last letter was heroic. I especially appreciated the exposition, in your own words, of the idea of Communion of Saints. I don't go along with you in all that you say, but now I understand much better why you Catholics feel that you can pray to the saints who have passed over to the other side. Thank you!

I don't care much if you fall behind in your ironing, but I worry about your piano-practicing. The daily demands on your time, especially your job away from home, may make it advisable for you to take longer to answer. You seem to prefer to write on Sunday; and if, like me, you need a few days for gestation ("simmering" is the word I customarily use, but I'd better not in connection with this correspondence — the connotation of coming to a slow boil is unfortunate), you may want to hold off until the next productive Sunday before dashing to get your letters into the mail.

Thank you for letting me read *The Woman Shall Conquer.* I am returning it right away as evidence that I do return books. (There are some people in my past whom I remember chiefly because of the books they have of mine.) Ware is a bit annoyed with us for continuing to mention publication of our letters: he feels that anything which interferes with our direct, person-to-person exchange is distracting. Not being the sort of writer we are, he doesn't understand that we can't write a grocery list without secretly hoping it will be published. (By the way, are you acquainted with the remarkable Catholic science-fiction novel, *A Canticle for Leibowitz* by Walter M. Miller, Jr.? It features a delicatessen list as a saint's relic. I'll be glad to lend you my copy if you're interested.) My own feeling about our referring books to each other is that we should; we are both readers. We shall both be reading things on the side anyway, so why not share with each other the best that we are reading? I envision such reading as one of the resources we can bring to our dialogue. When you send me books, just indicate the ones you want back in a hurry, the ones you use for reference for your column. For several weeks I have been wanting to send you two books of ours, which you may keep for quite a while, if you wish. I prefer to send you nothing polemic. You have less time than I to read, and anything I send will be, hopefully, the sort of thing that will enrich you, the sort of thing I want to share because I love it.

Such a book is Baron Von Hügel's *Letters to a Niece.* Here is a great Roman Catholic layman and scholar serving as intellectual and spiritual adviser to his Anglican niece, Gwendolen Greene, years before she herself became a Roman Catholic. You will find three sets of readers' markings in the book — those of my husband, my friend F. S. C., who is a saint in heaven but to whom I do not pray, and myself. If you want to add any underlinings or comments, I suggest you use a different colored pencil. I love carrying on conversations with people through books. F. S. C. willed her religious books to me. I feel that I can recapture her presence just by reading her exclamations and underlinings. (Although I do not pray to my friend, I pray for her, using the form on page 598 of our *Prayer Book:* "Almighty God, we remember this day before thee thy faithful servant Fredericka, and we pray thee that, having opened to her the gates of larger life, thou wilt receive her more and more into thy joyful service; that she may win, with thee and thy servants everywhere, the eternal victory; through Jesus Christ our Lord. Amen." If she wants to pray for me, that's her business; I'll do my praying straight to God.)

I asked you about hymn-singing because I was under the impression not much of it was done congregationally in your Church, and I was puzzled about the great wealth of hymns in our hymnal which are obviously Roman Catholic in origin. We have more than 75 hymns translated from Latin, and in addition we have the English hymns written in the nineteenth century by such converts to Roman Catholicism as Frederick Faber (*Faith of Our Fathers* — er — a bit altered for use in our hymnal), Jane Eliza Leeson (*Saviour, Teach Me Day by Day*), Matthew Bridges (*Crown Him With Many Crowns*), and Henry Collins (*Jesus, My Lord, My God, My All*). The *Te Deum* is my constant companion, and I say it almost every time I enter the church and kneel to pray before a service (*Prayer Book*, page 10). The other book I am sending you is a copy of our hymnal, which is the most ecumenical book I know. Poke around in the index of authors, translators, and sources, and you will find a treasure trove of Catholic poetry. Of course we have a lot of good Protestant hymns too, as well as many Anglo-Catholic and Greek Catholic. I read once that our Church (the Episcopal, part of the Anglican Communion) is like the child of divorced parents, loving both, grieving that they don't seem to be able to get together again. Certainly in our hymnal we reflect our double heritage. You will notice that our music, too, draws heavily on Roman Catholic sources, especially on plainsong. Among the more modern hymns I suggest you try the three by Jan Struther and the one by Lesbia

Scott, *I Sing a Song of the Saints of God,* which has become a universal children's favorite in the Episcopal Church and which your children may enjoy too.

From time to time I shall be asking you questions about the customs of your Church, not to fight with you about them, but to find out things I don't know. Such was my question on hymnody. I hope your Church will rediscover the joys and comforts and strengths to be found in congregational singing. Last Sunday I went with Ann, our seven-year-old, to visit the Assembly of God Church on the reservation. Although I have come to prefer the Episcopal form of worship to any other, I find that I can worship God in many different ways, and I find the Holy Spirit working through Christians of every stripe from Roman Catholic to Quaker. Ann had never been to a Pentecostal service before. She didn't care for the service. She is used to a great deal more form, and she found the music too "jumpy." The congregation sang the lively gospel hymns loudly, to the accompaniment of an accordion and a guitar, and I joined in with a right good will. Our hymnal and the Assembly of God songbook contain a few hymns in common, but the purpose of the compilers of the two books was obviously different. Our hymnal is more reflective; theirs is more emotional.

I've visited a Roman Catholic chapel on the reservation too. This was early last fall, before I began writing to you. My reaction at the end of the service was, "Now I see why they won't let their people go to a service at our church. They're afraid of the competition. Our service is very similar to theirs, but the people can understand ours and take part in it." I realize now that from your point of view such a thought on my part was uncharitable and grievously erroneous. Your Church states its reasons for not letting its people join in public worship with others. They sound to me like the East Berliners' rulers' reasons for not letting their people go to West Berlin. This restriction on worshiping with others is a wall your Church has built to keep its people in. A more secure and self-confident Church would give its people freedom to go anywhere they chose, knowing they would return. Fear, not faith, builds walls of restriction.

Maybe the Latin of the Mass seemed more incongruous out in the midst of an Indian reservation than it would in a city. A few white ranchers had missals, but all the Indians who were present were left without any understanding or interpretation of what was going on. (Our Church provides prayer books and hymnals for all worshipers and expects them all to join in the responses, the Creed, the General Confession, the canticles, and the hymns.) I realize that your view of the Mass is different from our view of the Holy Communion, but I don't think God's native tongue is Latin and I don't see why the people may not get some benefit from hearing the words which the priest addresses to Him. I cannot help recalling that the origin of the phrase "hocus-pocus" is in the Latin of the Mass (*Hoc est Corpus Meum*), and I hate to see sacred things becoming a meaningless jumble because of this hanging on to a language which was first brought into the Church because it was the vernacular of the time. It is ironic to me that St. Jerome first translated the Bible into Latin so that the people of his time and place could read it in their own language, and that your Church has solidified all its official expression into that language which is no longer vernacular for anybody.

Don't get me wrong about Latin. I happen to be for it as a language well worth studying. Right now I'm taking a university correspondence course in Latin, trying to get Hannibal over the Alps. Latin, however, lacks the grace and fluidity and much of the beauty of Greek, the language in which the New Testament was written. For example, in 2 Corinthians 1:19, 20, Latin doesn't even have a word for *yes*. It has to say *est*, "it is," which really isn't the same as *yes*. The Greeks had a word for it.

Is your service of baptism read in Latin? Is baptism usually private (in the presence of the immediate family and godparents) or in the context of a public service? Formerly in our Church the custom was to have baptism as a separate service, attended only by relations and godparents, but the tendency in many parishes now is to incorporate the baptism service in one of the regular Sunday morning services, with the whole congregation as witnesses to the entrance of a new member into the Church.

I meant to be gentle and irenic this time. I "threw the book at you" last time, not because you had stung me, but because you had reassured me that I needn't worry about hurting your feelings or making you mad. I've probably made you mad this time too, and I'm sorry. But I think what I've been saying is fairly representative of Protestant thinking. I've been putting off telling you my reaction to the Sharkey book because I want to be nice, but I guess I'd better deal with it now.

In spite of your statement that the Catholic Church never will make Mary a goddess, I find a strong tendency in that direction in such a paragraph as the following from Sharkey: "Christ always prefers to work in co-operation with His Mother. He is the Redeemer; she is the Co-redemptrix. He is the new Adam; she is the new Eve. We honor His Sacred Heart; we honor her Immaculate Heart. He is our King; she is our Queen."* This sort of thinking, and the thinking that pervades this book, is foreign to the spirit and the message of the New Testament. No scriptural or historical evidence whatever exists on which to base the doctrines of the Immaculate Conception or the corporeal Assumption of the Blessed Virgin Mary. For your Church to have "developed" such doctrines as late as 1854 and 1950 and to require Christians to believe them is repellent to anyone who does not accept the dogma of papal infallibility, which is itself a suspiciously recent development, having first been registered in 1870.

The fact that the Roman Catholic Church alone claims to be infallible is not enough to make me believe that she is or to forsake for her my Church, which admits it can make mistakes. Again I sense that your Church has wandered from the spirit and the message of the New Testament. Your Church gets around my objection by saying it alone is competent to interpret the New Testament. I again disagree. This is the classic tension between Catholic and Protestant viewpoints, between dictatorship and democracy. I do not believe in the individual's blind and ignorant interpretation of Holy Scripture. I have done what I could to prepare myself to interpret it intelligently. I have

* Don Sharkey, *The Woman Shall Conquer* (Milwaukee: Bruce, 1952), p. 232.

studied Greek in order to know the New Testament as it was written. I regularly consult the best biblical scholarship of our generation and of past generations. Sometimes my study of the Bible leads me to disagree with the traditions and practices of my own Church. When it does, I am free to speak out. The principle of self-criticism and the practice of listening to the criticism of others is, in my opinion, a very healthy one. Stifling self-criticism and turning a deaf ear to others' criticism is unhealthy and dangerous for an individual or an institution.

Nothing in the New Testament indicates to me that Christ promised infallibility to an institution. He doesn't seem to have been much of an Organization Man Himself. He gathered a group around Him and taught them intensively. He sent some followers out two by two. He spoke of building a Church, but He left no blueprint. He commended Peter for his affirmation, "Thou art the Christ, the Son of the Living God," and indicated He would build His Church on this rock of belief (both the Greek and the Latin indicate that Jesus was making a distinction between the masculine name *Peter,* meaning "rock," and the feminine noun *petra,* referring to Peter's statement of belief). Shortly after commending Peter, Jesus found him a stone of stumbling and had to say, "Get thee behind me, Satan," when Peter rebuked Him for referring to His coming death. Peter had a certain prominence in the early Church as we see it forming in the Acts of the Apostles, but there is no indication in Scripture, and I again find it inconsistent with the spirit of our Lord, to suppose that any "primacy" would be handed down to Peter's successors. My experience has been that the Spirit of God shows up in some unlikely places and that He is not necessarily transmitted by the laying on of hands — although, as you must know, by the grace of God the Apostolic succession has never been broken in the Episcopal Church either. (One of your Popes got around to declaring Anglican orders invalid in 1896; but we don't agree with your Church that it can make up its own rules and expect everybody else to play by them.)

Oh, dear. This isn't a bit irenic. Am I being brutal again? I want to understand you, but the more I understand sometimes, the madder I get. I feel I was unfair in bringing up the Devils of Loudun because they aren't in standard reference works. I don't know whether they (the book about them, I mean) are on your Index, but the book, by Aldous Huxley, is a scholarly, well-documented work, fascinating to read. It was not written as an attack on your Church. I think the book may have been reissued as a paperback recently, and I shall try to find it. I also intend to buy the paperback *Dark Night of the Soul.* I read parts of it in college but would get more out of it now.

Ralph Linton, the anthropologist, once told us a true story about saints that I think you will enjoy as part of our discussion. (I don't know whether this has been published; he told it to Ware and me at a tea in New York many years ago.) We were discussing Christian missions and the contribution that anthropology can make. He told us that the people of Madagascar, who worshiped their ancestors, were more favorably inclined toward the Roman Catholic missionaries than toward the Protestants because the Roman Catholics were generous to the point of sharing their ancestors (the saints), while the Protestants kept theirs to themselves. They suspected the Protestants of holding out on them!

In your last letter you say that Protestants developed a doctrine mainly in order to differ from the Catholic Church. I believe you were sincere in thinking such a thing, but I must assure you that Protestants don't operate that way. Sure, there may be some individual Protestants who are anti-Catholic unreasonably, but you will not find Protestant theologians working from any other motive than the quest for truth and the desire to know and do the will of God. My own impression, which may be unfair but is honest, is that the Roman Catholic Church sometimes develops its doctrines out of a will to power. I am inclined to agree with the English Roman Catholic Lord Acton that "All power tends to corrupt; absolute power tends to corrupt absolutely." Of course he lived in a time when it was possible to be a loyal Catholic and still be hostile to the dogma of papal infallibility. After the dogma became official, he stopped writing in opposition to it. I'm sure he did not stop thinking.

I have indicated my belief that the individual believer has the right (and I also believe it is a duty) to exercise his own intelligence and scholarship in reading and interpreting Holy Scripture. You believe that only your Church has the authority to say what is meant by any passage. My own feeling is that most passages speak for themselves and need no interpretation, but that a Church which needs to explain its divergences from Scripture would have to claim the sole right of interpretation. Some reason, for example, must exist 'way back in the history of your Church to have caused it to abandon the practice of administering Holy Communion in both kinds. Paul's comments on Holy Communion indicate that during his time the Church included both eating and drinking in the sacrament (1 Cor 11). Our Lord, in His words of institution, said, "Drink ye all of this" — the "all" being plural and referring to the "ye." In this instance the Protestant Churches have gone back to the earliest known tradition for this service, the tradition we find in the New Testament, while the Catholic Church has apparently substituted its own reasoning or expedience in withholding the wine from its communicants. Another example of the disregard for the words of our Lord and for the spirit of His teaching is the calling of your priests "Father." (Here I'm stepping on Episcopalians' toes too. A considerable number of priests of the Episcopal Church prefer to be called "Father.") This practice is directly contrary to Jesus' teaching as recorded in Matthew 23:1–12. I'll have none of it, is my attitude toward any such violation of His words. Again He said, "Use not vain repetitions," and as an example of the way to pray, suggested the prayer beginning, "Our Father." I have a feeling He would turn over in His grave (if He were in His grave) at the repetitive, unthinking use of the "Our Father" that goes on, not only in your Church, but in Protestant Churches and in public meetings across the land.

I don't like to be "throwing the Book — the Good Book — at you" again. I don't like the use of "proof texts." I'm inclined to agree with the Bible teacher Lucy Steele, who says, "A text without its context becomes a pretext." But I am not, in my own thinking, just pulling Bible verses out and holding them up. I am considering them all in their contexts and in the spirit of the message of the New Testament and the Lord to whom the New Testament bears witness. I cannot believe that your Church has any Christian tradition older or more reliable than the witness of the New Testament. Traditions which developed in centuries after the New Testament was written, especially traditions which refer to supposed historical fact occurring in New Testament times (such as the Immaculate Conception and the Assumption of Mary) are less reliable, from any reputable historian's viewpoint, than the earlier traditions, which the Church took care to record in the books of the Canon which it later accepted. Any conscientious reading of the entire New Testament will indicate that devotion to Mary had no place whatsoever in the early practice of the Christian Church. Maybe in this age of "Mom" there is a psychological need for a female-type god; but not in the venerable Hebrew-Christian tradition to which I hold.

Wow. I keep wanting to be constructive and then find myself lashing out at you. Well, bear with me. Maybe after I get all these negative thoughts ventilated, I can spend more time and space exploring with you our grounds of agreement. Your letters to me have caused me to respect, admire, and love you increasingly, but I am discouraged by the great gulf between us that doesn't seem any closer to being bridged. Let's keep praying.

With love,
BETTY

✝ ✝ ✝ ✝ ✝

CARLSBAD, NEW MEXICO

April 17

Dear Betty,

I am always so glad when your letter arrives: I wear out a path to the window watching for the mailman for a week before.

(He doesn't usually come until about 3:30, a horrible time because it leaves me in suspense all day and then I hardly have time to do more than glance at the mail before leaving for my hospital job.)

I'm so happy that you approve of our sending books to each other. You know, I have a buoyant feeling that we are getting somewhere, in spite of the gulf you feel between us yet. Here's why: up to now we have both, to a large extent, been fighting straw men. Most of the objections you have voiced to Catholicism have been based on misunderstanding, common to Protestants, of what the Church really does claim and teach. Similarly, my own ideas concerning Protestant theology have been based on my own mostly unthinking Protestant years and on what I have read from the Catholic viewpoint in the past eleven years.

To date it has seemed to me that we have been principally occupied with your criticisms of Catholicism as it appears to you and my attempts to correct your misconceptions by explaining the logic behind the doctrines (i.e., communion of saints) or by delineating the limits of the Church's actual teaching on dogmas you have misunderstood (i.e., papal infallibility). What I have done so far in this regard any good book of apologetics could have done better, though without the personal touch. I have consciously followed your lead, trying to answer the points raised in each letter and deliberately leaving it up to you and the Holy Spirit where we would go next.

Now, however, I have a rather exciting sense of being at a junction of two roads. We can go on as we have been, or we can take a short cut. The latter, I think, would enrich our interpersonal exchange because it would eliminate most, if not all, of the shadows and we could concentrate on real issues. To this end I am sending you Volume I of *Radio Replies*, a question-and-answer book from which I help myself liberally in explaining any doctrine of the Church to non-Catholics. I think you'll find it challenging. Father Rumble (or Carty?) may infuriate you at times (although his answers are models of meekness compared to the insolence of some of the questions) but he won't bore you. I would suggest that you start at the beginning and read straight through; I did, some years ago. It is a reference book I refer to frequently and the children too, for debates in school, etc., so I'll need it back, but there are three volumes in the series and I can spare one at a time. There is some overlapping in the volumes but not too much; any question that isn't treated in this one is practically sure to be treated in one of the others.

There are full explanations of most of the points you brought up in your last letter: like why we call our priests "Father" (didn't St. Paul tell the Corinthians "in Christ Jesus, by the Gospel, I have begotten you"?). And whether Christ referred to Peter's name or his declaration of faith. (Christ did not speak in either Latin or Greek but in Aramaic — and in Aramaic the words for Peter and "rock" are identical, *Cephas.* In fact, this was St. Paul's way of referring to Peter. Cf. 1 Cor 1:12). And the validity of Anglican orders. And the historical basis for the "development" of doctrines; they were not "developed" in 1854 or 1870 or 1950 but *defined;* they had been held, implicitly at least, since apostolic times. And why so little reference is made to Mary in the New Testament and the significance of what is there. And why Holy Communion is presently received under the one kind. And about "vain repetitions" in prayer.

Do you agree with me that we have reached the point in our dialogue where we can take that short cut and commune on a different level? Surely any potential reader who has followed us this far will not be put off; the well-instructed Catholic reader is already familiar with both the objections and the answers, and the Protestant reader who is really seeking more information can be referred to *Radio Replies* or dozens of other similar books which will explain what the Church teaches and why more thoroughly and authoritatively than I can do in these letters. What do you think?

The reason I'd like to get these questions out of the way is to be able to concentrate on something much more interesting, to me — the more valid criticisms you make of the Church, or, at least, of the "present discipline of the Church," to use Von

Hügel's phrase. I do agree with you (are you surprised?) that the principle of self-criticism and the practice of listening to the criticism of others is a very healthy one — within certain boundaries — and that turning a deaf ear to others' criticism is unhealthy and dangerous for an individual or an institution. And I found a couple of your most recent criticisms extremely thought-provoking and am interested in exploring them further. Your comment that the Church's reasons for not letting her people join in public worship with others sound to you like the East Berlin rulers' reasons for not letting their people go to West Berlin and that "a more secure and self-confident Church would give its people freedom to go anywhere they chose, knowing they would return" sounds very logical. In fact, I read that part of your letter over the telephone to a very good Catholic friend of mine and she agreed with you, citing her own experience when, with a teen-ager's curiosity and disregard for authority, she deliberately attended a couple of services at Protestant churches and felt them "empty" and practically meaningless in comparison with the Mass.

You see, our Mass is so sublime and so profound that it is almost impossible to convey to non-Catholics the difference between it and Protestant worship services. We have an altar, as St. Paul says, and upon it we offer God to God, through a valid renewal of the essence of the Last Supper — the turning of wine and bread into the Body and Blood of Christ — with Christ Himself, the Divine Priest and simultaneously the Divine Victim, offering the Sacrifice of His own Body and Blood on Calvary for the redemption of mankind and applying the graces obtained there to all those participating worthily in the renewal of that oblation.

I know, the Episcopalian and Lutheran services retain a similar form and motive; but because both have lost the apostolic succession and hence the power to effect the transubstantiation of the bread and wine into the actual Body and Blood of Christ, their services are only symbolic of the actuality of the Holy Sacrifice of the Mass. And the other Protestant bodies reject even the symbolism and their services are instructional, emotional, companionable get-togethers; they neither pretend to have nor to understand the need for *sacrificial* worship.

So why would Catholics wish to attend worship services in other churches? I can't imagine the early Christians being tempted to assist in heretical services; St. Paul did find it necessary to warn them to avoid heretics. The fact that in the eyes of the Church, most non-Catholic Christians today are only *material* and not *formal* heretics and are in good faith, and hence God accepts their worship to His glory and uses their services for the sanctification of the participants, does not make those services acceptable for Catholics.

However, there are always the curious, the rebellious, the poorly instructed, the weak Catholics who fear offending their neighbor more than offending God, who might decide to visit other churches; and because of the scandal such visits could occasion — implying, as they do, indifference to doctrines fundamental in Catholicism and rejected by separated Christians — the Church has explicitly forbidden such participation in the hope that the prohibition would restrain those whose ignorance or weak faith would not.

I found Baron von Hügel enthralling and am so grateful to you for sending the book. I don't know why I've never heard of him (or if I have, it hasn't registered). I agree with his belief that all religions manifest God, in varying degrees. This is compatible with the statement of Pope Pius IX in his encyclical to the bishops of Italy, August 10, 1863: "It is known to us and to you that those who are in invincible ignorance of our most holy religion, but who observe carefully the natural law, and the precepts graven by God upon the hearts of all men, and who being disposed to obey God, lead an honest and upright life, may, aided by the light of divine grace, attain to eternal life; for God who sees clearly, searches and knows the heart, the disposition, the thoughts and intentions of each, in His supreme mercy and goodness by no means permits that anyone suffer eternal punishment who has not of his own free will fallen into sin."

However, I am rather tentative about accepting von Hügel's

thesis that persons should be left where they are and deepened and strengthened in what they've got, rather than led to the fullness of Catholic truth. This is something I intend to try to think out further. The Baron's lovely gentleness in regard to those of other faiths is very different from Father Rumble's uncompromising exposition of the falsity of the various Protestant positions.

The Baron's comment about all converts being proselytizers at first struck home: I have attempted, without noteworthy success, to interest various persons in looking into the "credentials" — as Father John A. O'Brien, the great convert-maker, calls them — of the Church, because my own reaction on discovering the Catholic religion was "But why haven't any of the Catholics I've known *told* me about this?" Perhaps von Hügel is right in feeling that one should wait until others indicate that they have been called by the Holy Spirit to higher things. Actually, after the first few weeks when I wrote long letters to various relatives, explaining why I had become a Catholic and endeavoring to interest them in reading the books that had convinced me, I have very rarely taken the initiative in any discussion of religion. I do pray constantly and fervently for the conversion of a great many individuals, including yourself and my "scientologist" music teacher and my good Baptist boss and my obstetrician and my husband and parents and in-laws and practically everybody else who has ever shown any curiosity about my being a Catholic. According to Baron von Hügel's philosophy I might do better to pray for the deepening of what each one already has. But they lack so much! — How can I not want all of you to have *all* that Christ came to give His followers, so much of which can be found only in the Roman Catholic Church?

But let me get back to your letter. I wasn't too surprised that you found the Sharkey book "foreign to the spirit and message of the New Testament." Like a stew with too many ingredients, I suppose it was bound to give you indigestion. There are Catholics who don't like it either — usually the cold, intellectual, unemotional types who are embarrassed by sentiment and repelled by anything that smacks to them of superstition or overcredulity. They're just modern St. Thomases; Christ loves them too, though He did say: "Blessed are they who have not seen, and yet have believed."

In this connection I'd like to quote a Catholic editor, Stephen Oraze:

> The Catholic Church does not require that we believe information or predictions based upon private revelation, even though approved. But such revelation has its proper place in the Church and in our individual lives. The proof of much private revelation often comes, not so much from the ecclesiastical approval granted, as it does from the events actually taking place as predicted. So, when a message of warning is reportedly given from Heaven for the benefit of the people of earth, and the proof does come as predicted, then we would be foolish indeed to ignore the proof. . . .
>
> St. Paul, in his First Epistle to the Thessalonians 5:20 cautions: "Despise not prophecy."
>
> St. Thomas Aquinas, in his *Summa,* states that private revelations have their proper place in governing the course of Church actions. He says they are not given to prove the truth of Catholic doctrine, or add anything to its Articles of Faith. Rather, they are intended to provide, according to the current circumstances and needs of the times, suitable directions to guide and govern human actions.
>
> In other words, although all "public revelation" ended with Scripture, Almighty God in His mercy deigns to appear or send His Blessed Mother or other messengers from Heaven from time to time in order to provide guidance and direction to combat some particular problem of that time . . . or to grant special favors to their children on earth. . . . In most cases, private revelations are given to warn the people of the dangers against Christianity, the plans of the enemy, and the best means of combatting. . . .*

Dale Francis, who reads Protestant publications regularly, said in one of his columns that they carry frequent articles about religion among the Mexican people, and that whenever they mention the devotion to Our Lady of Guadalupe, which they can't ignore as it is everywhere in Mexico, they inevitably dis-

---

* *Divine Love,* Autumn, 1958.

miss it as superstition and treat it as if it takes away from love for Christ. But what are the facts? Our Lady appeared to a poor Indian widower, 57-year-old Juan Diego, on Tepeyac Hill near Mexico City in 1531, just ten years after the Spaniards conquered Mexico, telling him to go to the Bishop and convey her request for a shrine on that spot. When the Bishop insisted upon a "sign," she showed Juan some gorgeous roses (in December!) which he picked and she arranged in his tilma. When the roses were presented to the Bishop, the tilma was found to contain a magnificent portrait of our Lady as she had appeared to Juan Diego, painted on the coarse cloth. The picture is still there, hanging in the shrine, intact and beautiful after more than 400 years.

There were miracles, as there always are when our Lady appears among men, to signify God's approval. But the greatest miracle, as Frances Parkinson Keyes noted in *The Grace of Guadalupe,** "lay in the immediate flowering of faith":

> Until then, those who had freely and willingly accepted the doctrine brought them by the Frailes were few and far between. Many of the Indians had hidden in the hills at the missionaries' approach; others had slunk sullenly away to their homes. Now that two of their own people had received special signs of grace — one through revelation, the other through revival [an Indian miraculously cured after being shot in the throat with an arrow during the first public procession with the miraculous picture] — all this was changed. They were no longer crushed by a sense of racial inferiority and by formless fears; they were encouraged, uplifted, inspired. The priests were hard put to baptize all those who came flocking to them. Fonts were raised, even in desert places, to accommodate the multitude who could not quickly reach the churches, and the churches were overflowing, also.

Or, to get closer to our time if not to our continent, take Fatima. I wish you'd do some more thinking about Fatima. How do you explain the prophecies regarding Russia? At the time of the apparitions at the Cova da Iria, Russia was a prostrate,

---

* New York: Hawthorn Books, Inc., 70 Fifth Ave., © 1941, 1953 by Frances Parkinson Keyes, p. 71. Reproduced by special permission.

defeated nation. Who but God could know that she would spread her errors throughout the world, that nations would be annihilated, etc.? The last of the monthly appearances of our Lady to the children occurred on October 13, 1917; the Bolshevists gained control of the Russian government on November 3, three weeks later. How do you explain the "Miracle of the Sun"? You can't call it mass hallucination, because people miles away who knew nothing of what was taking place witnessed it. You might call it preternatural and attribute it to the devil, who can admittedly work signs and miracles to deceive even the elect — but "by their fruits you shall know them!" Satan would hardly be urging people to mend their ways and do penance and cease offending God. He couldn't be behind the mass reconversion of the Portuguese people which in a few short years transformed Portugal from an increasingly atheistic, anticlerical nation into a devoted, peaceful people who, by God's grace, were not even involved in World War II.

Christ came for all, not just for the learned men who would rather try to define the Trinity than become as little children, forgetting that God has His ways of putting the mighty down from their thrones and exalting the lowly. There are Catholics who look down their noses at private revelations and the devotion to Mary which is so much a part of simple people's faith. They wish, as Father Faber wrote a century ago, "to make Mary so little of a Mary that Protestants may feel at ease about her." In order to do this, they have to ignore the fact that it is Mary rather than Christ who has shown herself to these "little ones" so often; it is no wonder they love her. But her purpose is always to draw them — us — closer to Christ. He is the end; she is the means.

I have *A Canticle for Leibowitz*, thanks. I liked it, except for the business of the two-headed woman at the end, which I found obscure and repellent. I'm gathering up some books I think you'll enjoy. You didn't comment on my mention of *The Screwtape Letters* in an earlier letter, so I'll include it in case you haven't read it. I've got tracers out for my *Perfect Joy of St. Francis* and if I can locate it, it will go into the box. I'm also sending a biography of the Curé d'Ars and *My Beloved*, the story of a Carmelite nun, both of which I think you will enjoy reading. No big hurry about sending any of them back. Do you have the *Imitation of Christ?* It's such a classic that I expect you do. And have you ever read the *Confessions* of St. Augustine? That's another one I've got loaned out, but if you're interested I'll send it when I get it back.

I haven't had time to do anything with the hymnal except pick out the four pieces you recommended. The one by Lesbia Scott was right up my alley and I'm hoping to teach it to the kids.

Baptism in our parish is in English now, except for a few key parts which are said in Latin and then translated immediately. It is a private ceremony which takes place at the baptismal font near the entrance to the church, usually on Sunday afternoons but at other times for good reasons. In the restored Easter Vigil services there is a beautiful public renewal of the baptismal promises, conducted antiphonally between the priest and the entire congregation, in English, following which the priest sprinkles the people with the newly blessed Easter water as a reminder of their own baptism. The prayers, incidentally, for the blessing of the water are beautiful and significant. The priest prays that it may be "a fount of life, a water of new birth, a purifying stream . . . so that besides its natural power of cleansing bodies, it may have the effect of purifying souls. . . . May the power of the Holy Ghost descend into this brimming font, and may it make the whole substance of this water fruitful in regenerative power . . . may all stain of sin be wiped away . . . let human nature, created in Thy likeness and re-created to the honor of its maker, be cleansed of all ancestral defilement, so that every man who enters into this sacrament of regeneration may be born again into a new childhood of true innocence, Through our Lord Jesus Christ, Thy Son . . ."

It could possibly be that the Indians at the Catholic Mass you visited had more understanding of what was going on than you realized. I wouldn't feel too sorry for them. But facts like this do give added urgency to the liturgical renewal. One can come very close to God while kneeling in silence at Mass — you don't have to know what the priest is saying to know he is interceding with God for you, and to feel God's grace penetrating your soul. It is possible to answer all the responses and sing all the hymns in a vernacular service without ever really praying. Likewise, of course, it is possible to be bodily present at Mass with one's mind off on a thousand other things, or to derive abundant graces — "joys and comforts and strengths," to use your words — from congregational singing or almost any type of religious service.

I am enclosing a clipping of an interesting article on Christian unity published last August in the Catholic magazine *Extension,* written by an evangelical Protestant minister. The only thing that puzzles me is why Dr. Baxter isn't a Catholic. That's one thing I still can't understand about Protestants: I can see why they are Protestants when they have known nothing else, but how they can remain out of the Church once they have studied her claims with an open mind is a mystery to me.

Won't you be glad when we get to heaven where all these things that mystify and distress us now will be clearly seen as manifestations of God's love and mercy and wisdom? I can hardly wait.

I love Holy Week. The two and a half years I read the Breviary daily I was so steeped in the liturgy that external things seemed dreamlike. I felt the humility and divine munificence of Christ on Holy Thursday, washing the feet of His Apostles and then giving them His own Body and Blood — the desolation and heartrending grief of Good Friday as He was "led like a lamb to the slaughter" — the hushed, pregnant expectancy of Holy Saturday — and then the inexpressible, glorious joy of Easter Sunday morning. At that time, too, we had a pastor who scheduled Tre Ore services each Good Friday — three hours, from 12 to 3 p.m., with seven sermons (on the Seven Last Words) interspersed with responsive readings, psalms, hymns, prayers, etc. The Episcopal Church here has a similar service; do you? Our present pastor did not follow the custom, and I miss it, although it is likely I could not manage to go if he did.

Wishing you a happy, holy Easter! May God bless you and all your family.

Love,

LORRAINE

✓ ✓ ✓ ✓ ✓

ETHETE, WYOMING
April 24

Dear Lorraine,

It's been a lovely Easter. I have felt close to you this past week. At the same time I have been more than usually fragmented by the problems of other persons; I have lost my temper at Ware and nagged him, something I hate to do; I have screeched at the children. Sanctity seems a bit far off.

I appreciate and agree with your feeling that we have come to a junction. I'm more than willing at this point to take the short cut. We could feel around for months saying " 'T'ain't so" and "Oh, yes, it is" without getting anywhere. We can't even agree on many things that should be matters of factual knowledge. For instance I was amazed at your statement that St. Matthew's Gospel was written in Aramaic. After scurrying around in all the pertinent reference works I could find, I read that this had at one time been an opinion of scholars; and I assume it is still the opinion of Roman Catholic scholars, although the best Protestant scholars agree that the entire New Testament was written in Greek, with perhaps some Semitic-language source material used. Anyway, whenever the passage about Peter came into the Greek language, the Church's tradition must have indicated that a distinction should be made in that language between the masculine Peter and the feminine (or abstract) *petra*. In my reading I also learned that your Church's New Testament scholars are the only ones who fail to agree with all other New Testament scholars that the writing of Mark preceded the writing of Matthew and Luke.* These are matters to be determined by all sorts of evidence, to which you and I don't have access. There's not much point in our stubbornly defending opposite viewpoints of this sort. I'll read *Radio Replies*, all three volumes, but I'll have to ask you to read one of the Anglican question-and-answer books, *Answer Me This*, just so you'll know this sort of approach is not confined to your apologists. Moss makes me as mad at some points as he is going to make you at others. He doesn't speak for *me*, but he represents the thinking of quite a large number of Episcopalians. Perhaps reading his book will help you to see that some people have a strong, clear, and sincere reason for insisting on referring to your Church as *Roman* Catholic, not just Catholic. These people, who are devout Catholics themselves, are not motivated primarily by anti-Roman Catholicism. Of course I don't ask you to agree with them, but I ask you to listen to them and seek to understand them.

One thing that bothers me about *Operation Understanding* is that it is so one-sidely an attempt to get us to understand you with apparently no interest on your part in understanding us. True, the logic of your position would demand such an approach; but if Roman Catholics understood Protestants' viewpoints better, they could skip a lot of useless argumentation and get down to real issues. I keep feeling that the unity your Church seeks is the unity the lion seeks with the zebra. I'll admit our zebra has a shocking number of stripes. This is our problem as Protestants, and we cannot hope to approach Christian unity until the major Protestant divisions have been healed. Many of these divisions are senseless, based on national origins or temperamental differences. Others are serious but curable by God's grace.

I'm so glad you like von Hügel. I went through the book looking for your underlinings and enjoyed the conversation. His attitude toward others is so deeply charitable that I love to read and reread his letters. I feel loved through them. For me the Word must become Flesh. Not arguments but persons have

* Most Catholic New Testament men, as I've been informed, agree the Greek Mark preceded the Greek Matthew. Cf. Wikenhauser, *New Testament Introduction;* Stanley, "Gospel of Matthew," in *New Testament Reading Guide.*

been most deeply influential in my life — most radiantly the Person of Jesus Christ, and after Him the legions of followers, the ones I've known through books, such as von Hügel's, and the ones I've known face to face. The attitude in von Hügel that you question — "That the presumption is always in favour of souls remaining, as to institutional appurtenance, where they are — it being God's affair to make it clear to them if, doing their best where they are, He wants them elsewhere" — is congenial to my own thinking as it has developed in the past several years. It is one reason I prefer to use the "hold-up" prayer for persons with whom I disagree. I don't think I have any right, for example, to pray for your conversion, and I question your right to pray for mine. I was converted, a long time ago, to faith in the Lord Jesus Christ. Since then I have changed my "institutional appurtenance," but I have kept my faith in the Lord Jesus Christ.

I have come to feel that full acceptance of another person — as he is, not as he could be — is basic to Christian interpersonal relationships. My motto as a wife is, "Love him — and let him be." By "let him be" I do not mean, "leave him alone." I mean, "let him *be*" — himself, as he is. To love "the self that he can be" is to love nothing. One of the greatest discoveries of my life has been that God loves me — as I am. He wants me to be the person He had in mind when He made me, but He loves me now, as I am. "No matter what," I said to Sarah, our oldest, the other day when I was assuring her of God's love for her now. "No matter what?" she asked with almost incredulous relief. "No matter what," I assured her. I mentioned early in this letter that the problems of other persons have been fragmenting me. These personal problems, involving members of the mission staff, have largely arisen because Christian persons have not been willing to accept each other as they are. I myself am far from being able to practice acceptance all the time. That's why I sometimes nag Ware and screech at the children.

It is wholly generous of you to want to share the riches you have found in your Church. Please keep on praying for me, but carefully consider von Hügel's attitude and, if you can come to accept it, lay off the prayers for my conversion.

I am returning *Screwtape Letters,* which I have. (It was very influential to me in high school.) A C. S. Lewis book which would be more germane to our conversation is *Pilgrim's Regress,* an allegorical spiritual autobiography which I don't have. I'll try to find a copy. I am also returning Volume I of *Radio Replies* because my next-door neighbor lent me this volume after you referred to it in an earlier letter of yours. You may send Volume II along and I'll read it. So far, instead of going straight through Volume I, I have skipped around with the index as a guide. I'm learning a lot about what your Church believes. I'd like to see Faber's *Spiritual Conferences,* and I believe I am going to enjoy the books about the Carmelite nun and the Curé d'Ars. Thank you for sending them. I have the *Imitation of Christ* but have never really read it; and I have the *Confessions* of St. Augustine but haven't gone far into them. Both are basic Christian classics, and I'm sorry I have neglected them. I'll try them anew. Are you acquainted with Evelyn Underhill's *Mysticism?* If not, I think you would enjoy it.

Yes, I'll be glad when we get to heaven. I think we'll all be considerably surprised as well as enlightened. Do you know C. S. Lewis' *The Great Divorce?* It's a thought-provoking treatment of heaven and hell, brief and fanciful.

The newspaper interview with you indicates that you are a member of the Third Order of St. Francis, the Legion of Mary auxiliary, and the Confraternity of Mary. What are these things? I gather from reading elsewhere that two of them probably provide you with a Rule of Life. If there's nothing secret about them, will you tell me what it means to be a member? I think there are similar orders in the Episcopal Church, but I've not come into contact with them.

In this letter I was going to try to explain my approach to the sacraments and also to complain a bit about some of the practical applications of your Church's attitude toward the Protestants; but I don't feel that I want to do either right now. Ware's parents are visiting us this week, and we shall also be entertaining a couple of extra clerics on Thursday, and I must make a talk on Indians to the American Association of University

Women meeting in Riverton, Friday. Special visitors and events have a way of coming all at once.

Love,

BETTY

✝ ✝ ✝ ✝ ✝

J. M. J.

CARLSBAD, NEW MEXICO

May 7

Dear Betty,

I feel like underlining the *dear*. The closeness you mention feeling has been reciprocated, only on this end it has been mingled with self-recriminations. I don't know when I've had so many "afterthoughts" about anything as about my last letter to you. I should have followed your advice and let it — can I say simmer? — longer; but it was early in Holy Week and there was so much housecleaning to be done and Easter preparations and other things demanding attention, and I was too eager to get the letter and the books on their way. As soon as I mailed it I began having all kinds of misgivings.

That phrase on the first page — "correcting your misconceptions" — that wasn't tactful, and the sentence would have been just as clear and more charitable without it. I worried about having used the word "heretic" later on.

I am very, very sorry you found my remark about praying for your conversion offensive. It's something else I had qualms about after I had sent the letter. I should probably explain that I don't ever really say in so many words, "O God, convert her!" I do fully subscribe to the attitude you expressed in your column about the hold-up prayer, that God knows what the other person needs and it isn't for us to try to tell Him. If any words form themselves in my mind at all, they are usually "*Bless her,* Lord!"

But so much goes into that simple phrase. It means: "Enrich her soul with Thy grace; increase her wisdom and charity and understanding; give her strength to bear whatever suffering Your Divine Providence permits to befall her and to grow closer to You through carrying her cross; and if it is Your will, O Lord, open her mind and heart to the fullness of Your Truth." My prayers for anybody else, as for myself, are always contingent on His will: if I am ever petitioning Him for anything contrary to His will I certainly don't want my prayer answered my way, but only His, and only when and as and if He wills it.

I find the same tendency in my letters to you that you criticize in *Operation Understanding* — the one-sided attempt to explain our position with less apparent interest on our part in trying to understand you. In *Operation Understanding* I think it is justified, because that is the purpose behind it: Dale Francis' idea was to send a Catholic paper to Protestant ministers to enable them to see from the Church's own publications what she really teaches and holds so they wouldn't be so apt to be misled by apostate priests, POAU-ers, and other non-Catholic "authorities" on Catholicism.

As regards our correspondence, however, I find the one-sidedness less excusable and can only say I'm sorry; I do read and weigh carefully and respect your viewpoint. I started to say something of the sort in my last letter, when I mentioned that my knowledge of Protestantism had been compounded from my own mostly unthinking Protestant years and what I had read and observed since becoming a Catholic. I was a Protestant because I was born into a Protestant family. Until about eighteen I accepted what I was taught in church and Sunday School and summer conferences without particularly doubting or questioning any of it. The influence of some agnostic college professors and my own superficial intellectuality led me to abandon, more or less, my childhood faith without any attempt to ascertain through personal study and investigation whether it was founded on rock or on sand. I can remember one of my favorite comments at college (which I considered clever and sophisticated) when the subject of religion came up: "Well, if there really is a God, don't you know He must be sitting up there laughing His head off at the messes we dopes keep getting ourselves into down here?" Of course I didn't realize then that I was falling into the very human error of projecting my own motives and weaknesses onto God, assuming that because I viewed with amused superiority the stupidities and mistakes of others, God — if there was a God — must be doing the same thing.

I had to learn at least the beginnings of humility before my faith in Christ returned — and I *was* humbled, in ways I won't go into here. I never really stopped praying to God, but for ten years I ignored Jesus completely. I remember one Easter morning hanging a washing on the line while my neighbors were going off to church. It was through an excellent, detailed Bible storybook that my mother-in-law found in an old trunk and passed on to me to read to Bob and Jerry that I came to see the sweep of history, the design, the pattern, in the Bible stories I had learned as a child. I read to them of the fall of Adam and Eve, the promise of a Redeemer, the falling away and penitent returning to God of the Chosen People, repeated over and over through the centuries, the fulfillment of the Old Testament prophecies in the New Testament, and the rejection of the Messias by the majority of the same chosen race, who never seemed to learn. My faith in Christ was restored; the buildup was gradual but the belief was a sudden, illuminating experience I shall never forget: one night in bed I suddenly knew that Jesus truly was the Son of God and the knowledge flooded me with joy and with gratitude to God for enlightening my darkness. I might have started attending Protestant services again and remained a Protestant the rest of my life, if it hadn't been for the letter-transfer business soon after our marriage that had left me not sure whether I was a Presbyterian or a Methodist.

A visit with my Church of Christ sister and brother-in-law soon after this stirred me to the realization that it *is* important to belong to the Church as well as to believe in Christ, and that it does make a difference which Church, because all can't be equally true. Ironically, it was a Church of Christ minister's sermon a few weeks later describing how the "original Church" had "apostasized" and turned away from the true faith and substituted "doctrines of men" for the teachings of Christ that led me into an argument with a Catholic friend, who insisted that if I was really sincere in seeking the true Church, I owed it to myself to hear the Catholic side as well.

What I'm getting at in this long digression is that through our correspondence I am growing in understanding and appreciation of a Protestant faith ("faith" not in the sense of a denomination but of an individual's beliefs) more "catholic" than I was previously familiar with, and I am grateful for the new dimension you have added to my understanding, as well as for the stimulation your questions and comments have provided in encouraging me to reexamine and reaffirm my own faith. I am afraid I have tended to classify Protestants into two main types: those like I used to be, who accept more or less passively the beliefs of whatever denomination circumstances have placed them in, taking a tolerant attitude to other churches with the feeling that "We're all heading for the same place anyway" — and those like my sister and the fundamentalist Baptists, Mormons, Jehovah's Witnesses, Seventh Day Adventists, etc., who are firmly convinced that they and they alone are right and everybody else is wrong.

There is one sentence in your last letter that intrigues me: "If Roman Catholics understood Protestants' viewpoints better, they could skip a lot of useless argumentation and get down to real issues." I would love to have you elaborate on that and be more specific. Would you? And I am awaiting with interest your promised discussion of your approach to the sacraments and your complaints about the practical aspects of our Church's attitude toward Protestants. While on the sacraments, I wish you would satisfy my curiosity on a couple of points: What disposal is made of the blessed bread that is left over from your Communion services? And is your husband "High" or "Low" Church, or somewhere in between? (Is he still with us in our dialogue?)

You inquired about the various things I belong to. The Third Order of St. Francis is a religious order for lay men and women who, while living in the world, strive after Christian perfection under the direction of Franciscan priests and in the spirit of St. Francis, by observing a Rule of Life designed to help them avoid sin, grow in grace and virtue, and promote works of Christian charity. The primary purpose is the sanctification of its members; the Popes have called it "a school of Christian perfection." There is only one meeting a month, but the Rule permeates our daily life. It has both negative and positive precepts, as you will see from the enclosed leaflet, and provides a simple, flexible framework within which any Catholic of good will can grow in holiness.

I'm still trying to find the Timmermans book on St. Francis. The last I knew, our novice mistress had it and passed it among her novices to read, but we have no novices at present and nobody seems to know who had it last. However, I will send Theodore Maynard's *Richest of the Poor,* which belongs to our fraternity library (we buy occasional books from our common fund and also receive donated books now and then) — and also G. K. Chesterton's *St. Francis of Assisi,* which is more of an essay than a biography.

The Legion of Mary is a much newer organization than the Third Order — exactly 700 years newer. Although it is not a religious order in the sense that the various third orders are — it does not have a Rule, a novitiate, habit, etc. — it has a similar dual purpose: the sanctification of its members and the bringing of Christ to society. There is a big difference in its operation. The Legion apostolate is founded on the weekly meeting, which lasts one hour and is divided about evenly between prayer and spiritual formation (the latter a brief instruction by the director), and the practical aspects of the apostolate (the reports of the members on work done during the previous week and the assignment of work for the coming week). Each member pledges at least an hour's apostolic work weekly. This is generally performed in pairs, on the gospel principle of sending disciples forth two by two, and may consist of any good work which the parish priest desires them to do: visiting the sick, distributing Catholic literature, assisting with the parish census, teaching catechism, and so on. Catholics who are in sympathy with the Legion's aims and methods but are unable to undertake the obligation of the weekly meeting and work assignments may become auxiliary members by being duly enrolled and by offering specified daily prayers, including five decades of the Rosary and the *Magnificat*, for the success of the Legion apostolate. In our parish we do not have a senior praesidium (the Legion has adopted the Roman military names for its groups, as being symbolic of the courage, discipline, honor, endurance, and loyalty required of those who serve as soldiers — Legionaries — of Jesus and Mary). We do have junior praesidia under the direction of the Sisters at the junior high, and it was thus I became affiliated as an auxiliary member.

The Confraternity of Mary, Queen of All Hearts, is going to be harder to explain, because I am fairly sure from our past correspondence that you will neither understand nor approve. No meetings, no contributions, no officers, no Rule — it is a purely spiritual fellowship of those who have consecrated themselves to Jesus through Mary by the formula of St. Louis De Montfort and are determined to live that consecration by always acting *with* Mary — never doing anything for God or souls on our own, but always with a sense of union of our will with hers; *in* Mary — looking at everything through her eyes, taking on her views and values; *through* Mary — going to God through her, as He sent Jesus to us through her; and *for* Mary — ultimately for God, of course, but knowing that everything we do to please her pleases the Blessed Trinity. This is nothing to be taken lightly: one prepares long and carefully before making this consecration, and living by it transforms one's whole life.

I will send you a copy of *Queen of All Hearts*, the magazine published by the Montfort Fathers for the express purpose of spreading this devotion. This particular issue (September-October, 1960) contains an article I wrote (p. 11) tucked in among other articles and features, mostly written by priests, explaining various theological aspects of the De Montfort consecration. It'll probably give you nightmares. Non-Catholics are always so afraid any honor paid to Mary takes something away from the honor due to Christ.

Anyway . . . those are the three organizations I belong to.

There is nothing in any of them incompatible with the others; they dovetail nicely. The Third Order provides me with a Rule to live by and makes me a member of the great family of Franciscans, over 300 of whom have been named saints or beati of the Church in the past 700 years. The Legion of Mary auxiliary membership enables me to assist with my prayers and moral support and share in the merits of one of the youngest and most apostolic lay organizations in the Church. Underlying the other two and coloring all that I do is my consecration to Jesus Christ through Mary, to whom (in the words of the consecration formula, renewed frequently) I have given "my body and soul, my goods, both interior and exterior, and even the value of all my good actions, past, present, and future; leaving to (her) the entire and full right of disposing of me and of all that belongs to me, without exception, according to (her) good pleasure, for the greater glory of God, in time and in eternity."

Thanks for sending *Answer Me This*. I haven't read it yet. I dropped Father Klister, editor of the *Southwest Catholic Register*, a note about it and the C. S. Lewis books and the Underhill book, which I am not familiar with, but haven't had a reply.

I'll send the *Spiritual Conferences*. On looking through the book it appears that I've only read parts of it myself — the essay on kindness and the one on spiritual reading, both of which I liked very much. I have a bad habit of starting books and getting distracted by some other reading before I've finished them and never getting back. Do you?

Sorry about the fragmentation. Here too. I have a convenient faculty for giving my whole attention to whatever I'm doing at the moment, whether it's writing, practicing the piano, cleaning house, sewing, talking with a friend, transcribing medical dictation, or whatever. It has both advantages and disadvantages. What I do, I do well — but what a lot gets neglected and left undone! Joe and the kids are always mad at me for one reason or another. I do pray for you. Pray for me.

With love,

LORRAINE

Ethete, Wyoming

May 20

Dear Lorraine,

I'm slow answering and am sorry. I've minded not getting around to writing you because it means I'll have to wait that much longer for your reply. This thing is automatically self-disciplining, isn't it?

Almost two weeks ago the Küng book (*The Council, Reform and Reunion,* New York, Sheed & Ward) came. (I have been so busy for the past ten days reading *my* books that I haven't begun to do justice to *yours.* Every time I wander through the study, I find another book that I think will throw light on our conversation. Also, it's been a time crammed full with visitors, official and unofficial; the Bishop came and confirmed Sarah and 17 other people; and Ann and Martha had birthdays.) The Küng book arrived on a Monday. Your latest letter came the following Wednesday, the same day that I was to speak to a church-women's group in Lander on "Famous Women in the Bible." An hour after Küng came, I had telephoned someone in the women's group to feel out the permissibility of switching topics and presenting "The Roman Catholic-Protestant Dialogue" instead. I had decided it might be fruitful to share selected passages from our letters, illuminating and expanding them with Küng. Then for the next two days, when I had the time, I read Küng. We spent all of Tuesday evening and all of Wednesday morning (except for 15 minutes when I sneaked to the post office, found your letter, and read it) entertaining some people who were interested in the work of the mission. They included the national church officer, a priest, who is in charge of Indian work. I fed four extra for lunch, and then we took off in our car for the Casper airport, 140 miles away, to get them to an airplane which was to leave there two and half hours after we finished lunch. I took Küng and our dialogue folder along and, on the return trip to Ethete, finished reading the former and marked the latter for reading to the group that evening.

I think it's interesting that we both picked about the same time to let others (not just a selected few) in on our dialogue. You have written a column describing what we are doing. I have opened up a lot of our thinking to a study group of mostly young Episcopal churchwomen. Without Küng to quote I should have considered it premature to present parts of our dialogue to a group. I am tremendously excited by this man's mind, his approach, his spirit. A great deal of what he says is applicable to our Church too: I think particularly of his description of dual dangers into which the Church may fall, the dangers of Sadduceeism (conformism, opportunism, modernism) and of Pharisaism (confessionalism, immobility, traditionalism), of being too worldly or too churchy (pp. 21–24). I love his use of the term "separated brethren" to describe us. It has a better ring than "heretics." (I don't mean this as a jab at you for using that word about my kind of people. I am just so very grateful for the whole tone of the Küng book that I like to go around quoting it at anybody who will listen.)

At least 15 of the 18 women who were present at the meeting that Wednesday night made a point of speaking to me afterward about what we are doing. They were tremendously interested, in spite of the fact that I read for more than an hour. Something I hadn't anticipated was the built-in interest stemming from the fact that many of these women have sisters or brothers who have married Roman Catholics. Bewilderment, inability to cope with the interpersonal problems that mixed marriages bring to a larger family group, and relief that here was somebody who could talk back to a Catholic were reflected in what they said after my talk.

A couple of the women wondered when we could possibly find the time to do the things we are doing. I said neither of us thought housework was the most important thing in the world; but when I say such things, I don't want to give the wrong impression. I'm not against cleanliness and order. The spokesman for the housekeepers that night went on to say that she might feel she should be spending some time reading and studying, but if she knew that a floor had to be waxed or clothes had to be ironed she just couldn't neglect those tasks. Well, I have the (perhaps slippery) philosophy that too much wax makes children fall down, and that sheets and blue jeans go just as well unironed. The writer of most of the meditations for our national Church magazine, *The Episcopalian,* has some comments on Martha and Mary which I think you would enjoy. She is Mary Morrison, and this is part of what she says:

> Anyone who wants to stir up a group of Church women need only mention the story of Mary, who sat listening to Jesus and earned His approval, and Martha, who plugged away at the housework and earned only a rebuke. . . .
>
> Perhaps it would sharpen our thought to retell the story, reversing only one detail — the attitudes of the two women. Jesus comes to the house: Martha is bustling about happily in the kitchen, enjoying her work, wholly focussed on the meal which her Lord is soon to enjoy. Mary is sitting at Jesus' feet — but is she hearing His word? Not at all, she is thinking that nobody should be so stupid as to want to be out in that stuffy old kitchen while the Master is talking. So she might say to Jesus, "Lord, dost thou not care that my sister faileth to heed Thy word? Bid her therefore that she listen." What would Jesus say? Well — we don't know that, but we can see clearly that of these two it is Kitchen Martha who is single-minded, while the distracted one is Mary, sitting at Jesus' feet though she may be.
>
> At its deepest level the story of Mary and Martha may speak to this point. Singleness, simplicity, a focussed mind: the "one thing needful" may be just that. It may be going one's own way, doing what one is doing as for the Lord, without fretting about what other people may or may not be doing. It may be developing that almost unknown talent of being oneself. . . .*

Being oneself — I think you have that talent, and I think I do too. Ware is a bit concerned about our dialogue's becoming a forum as a result of your writing about it in your column and inviting suggestions and comments. I believe we can be enough ourselves to retain the character of a dialogue while using all the

* *The Episcopalian,* July, 1960, p. 45. Reprinted with permission.

added resources that come our way and seem to fit what we are doing. Let us, however, be wary of suggestions from men about how to proceed. The Episcopal priest from Lander, who had heard my talk to the women, brought the Roman Catholic priest from Lander to see me a couple of days later. They were on their way to the hot springs swimming pool near here and dropped in for just a few minutes. The Episcopalian had told the Roman Catholic about our dialogue. He said he was aware of having read your name and added, "But frankly, when I see that some religious article has been written by a woman, I-er-make a point of not reading it." I understood his prejudice. I have a strong feeling that men and women are close to being different species in the way they think and arrive at the same truth by very different methods. (Most of the "mental cruelty" charges in the Hollywood "divorce" cases seem to stem from the fact that the man is a man and the woman is a woman.)

You ask whether my book-reading habits are like yours. I think so. In my very first letter to you I mentioned having dipped into a mystery thriller. I've never been back to it and probably won't unless I become too exhausted some day to get on with any of the other books in progress. Right now my bedside table has six of your books waiting insistently. (Volume II of *Radio Replies* is the only one I've started.) In addition, besides the Bible there's a paperback volume called *The Papal Encyclicals*, edited by Anne Fremantle, which I've been using for reference; and four other books I'm in various stages of reading: the Küng volume, which I am about to send you; Aldous Huxley's *The Devils of Loudun*, which I found in paperback and am rereading; Emil Brunner's *The Misunderstanding of the Church*, which is throwing a bright Protestant light; and Ronald Knox's *Enthusiasm, A Chapter in the History of Religion with Special Reference to the Seventeenth and Eighteenth Centuries*. Knox has a lovely preface, explaining that this book is the one on which he has worked with great care and devotion for more than 30 years; this, for him, is the Book. Then he says something that reminds me of the transformation that is being wrought in us as we come to know each other and each other's faith:

Those who cherished the belief that I was writing a refutation of all the heresies must be prepared for a disappointment; I have only dealt with certain selected points of view, they were not exactly heresies, and I have not refuted them.

To be sure, when the plan of the Book was first conceived all those years ago, it was to have been a broadside, a trumpet-blast, an end of controversy . . . here, I would say, is what happens inevitably, if once the principle of Catholic unity is lost! All this confusion, this priggishness, this pedantry, this eccentricity and worse, follows directly from the rash step that takes you outside the fold of Peter! All my historical figures, Wesley himself included, were to be a kind of rogues' gallery, an awful warning against illuminism. But somehow, in the writing, my whole treatment of the subject became different; the more you got to know the men, the more human did they become, for better or worse; you were more concerned to find out why they thought as they did than to prove it was wrong. . . .*

Oh! Another book beside my bed, a book which may be too deep for me but I am going to try, is Pierre Teilhard de Chardin's *The Phenomenon of Man.*

I'm sure you are free to read Küng and Knox. (But is *imprimi potest* a weaker endorsement than *nihil obstat* and *imprimatur?* Küng bears the former; Knox, the two latter.) What about Huxley and Brunner and Teilhard de Chardin? How does a lay person find out what is on the Index anyhow? I never see anything published about it, as Legion of Decency movie ratings are published. Do all priests have up-to-date Index lists? What do you think of Küng's opinion (pp. 180–181) that "A thorough reform (or even abolition) of the Index should be considered . . . a *warning* about a book, with solid grounds given for it, would be more effective than a prohibition against reading it without any statement of the reasons. Indeed, it would often be the case . . . that to allow free discussion would do more to clarify a problem and to set men's minds at rest than any hasty condemnation"?** I like what he says. For instance I think some

* Ronald Knox, *Enthusiasm* (New York: Oxford University Press, 1950), pp. v, vi.

** Hans Küng, *The Council, Reform, and Reunion* (© Sheed and Ward, Ltd., 1961. Published in the U. S. A. by Sheed & Ward, Inc., New York.)

things in Huxley's study of the Devils of Loudun will offend you, among them the equating of Hindu religious insight with revealed truth. Nevertheless, the book is scholarly (when the author is not digressing with his dogmatic philosophical opinions, which are easily distinguishable from the scholarship) and full of interest, especially past page 94. My interest in recommending it to you is to point out that mass hysteria is a religious and psychological and social phenomenon which has many aspects.

Would you be allowed to read Brunner on the Church? He believes that the Roman Catholic Church has departed radically from the early New Testament assembly of believers, which was a pure communion of persons and had nothing of the character of an institution about it.

Are you allowed to read the work of the Jesuit priest Pierre Teilhard de Chardin, who was forbidden during his lifetime to publish his book on the development of man? (I feel here the inconsistency of your Church's leaders, who are willing to admit Galileo's ideas as acceptable — from a safe distance of centuries — but who shy away from profound contemporary scholarship, even by a dedicated Catholic priest, because it suggests new and different ideas. Have they no confidence that all truth is God's, and that truth, placed side by side with error, will prevail?)

Of these three books which may be questionable from the Roman Catholic standpoint I should like especially to have you read Brunner's *The Misunderstanding of the Church*. I shall not send any of them unless you say I may. I don't think it's cricket for you to pray for my conversion; likewise I don't think it's cricket for me to try to undermine your confidence in your Church's authority if this is a cornerstone of your faith. Brunner has clarified and given words to some of my own strong feelings about the nature of the Church.

Connected with my feelings about the Church is my attitude toward the sacraments. I sense a sacramental quality in every meal that Christians share, whether within the family or in a larger group. I see something sacramental in two Christian housewives coming together for a morning coffee break. Holy Communion in the Episcopal Church is the central service. It has come to mean a great deal to me as something I have added to my host of sacramental experiences, but it has not replaced the others. I cannot accept the belief that Jesus, who once offered Himself upon the cross, is continually being reoffered in the Mass. I look upon the Holy Communion as a memorial, and also as a means of grace. I believe that I carry Christ within me, but not in my stomach. I eat and drink the bread and wine in remembrance that Christ died for me, that His blood was shed for me, and I feed on Him in my heart by faith, with thanksgiving.

You ask what disposal is made of the blessed bread that is left over. A rubric on page 84 of our *Prayer Book* directs, "And if any of the consecrated Bread and Wine remain after the Communion, it shall not be carried out of the Church; but the Minister and other Communicants shall, immediately after the Blessing, reverently eat and drink the same." The usual custom is for the priest himself to consume the consecrated elements. You have probably noticed that Article XXVIII includes the statement, "The Sacrament of the Lord's Supper was not by Christ's ordinance reserved, carried about, lifted up, or worshipped."

About baptism I tend to disagree with the Episcopal Church (and with the Presbyterian Church, in which I received most of my Christian nurture). A careful, prayerful acquaintance with the New Testament convinces me that baptism should follow repentance and should be administered only to those who are old enough to repent of their sins. I know all the arguments in favor of infant baptism, but they don't hold enough water for me. I think it's fine to have a service in which parents dedicate their infants to the Lord and themselves to bringing up their infants in the Christian fellowship. In our service of confirmation the believers, "having come to years of discretion," renew, ratify and confirm the vows that were made at baptism. Do yours? My impression is that the Roman Catholic Church goes in for confirmation generally earlier than ours does. Our own Bishop asks that young people to be confirmed be at least 12 years old and thoroughly instructed. Thus they are expected to know what is going on and to enter with full consciousness into their confirmation.

I don't mention my views on infant baptism to Episcopal priests. I go along with the custom. I don't expect to find an institutional Church that is perfect. I think it is my duty and privilege to work within the Church in which I find myself, to help it realize its mission as a fellowship of Christ. In another 100 years, if the Roman Catholic Church has the courage to renew itself according to the leading of the Holy Spirit, it may be in a position to call to the (by then, I hope, substantially reunited) "separated brethren" to come home. When I ask Roman Catholics to understand Protestants' viewpoints better, what I'm doing is asking you to understand that it is not through our stubbornness or our ignorance that we fail to heed the present call of your Church. Küng presents the case for renewal within your Church far better than I can. After reading him I was filled with an elated hope that some day we may indeed become one flock with one Shepherd, one Lord, one faith, one baptism. I am eager to know your reaction to the Küng book. When he says, near the very end, "It is quite unthinkable that after centuries of separation we could be reduced not only to a common denominator but to a single numerator," and calls for "unity in *diversity*, unity in a variety of rites, languages, customs, modes of thought and action and prayer," and says, "Such unity is more perfect than uniformity,"* my hope expands into the beginning of a faith that such unity is attainable. Maybe with such a unity you could even have your Confraternity of Mary, Queen of All Hearts.

The magazine you sent me tries valiantly to show that devotion to Mary is Christocentric. Throughout the Marian literature I have seen run two themes which distress me: one, that Christ is God and therefore unapproachable except through someone else such as Mary, "a creature like ourselves." (Related to this theme is the recurring threat that Mary has a terrific task of holding back the judgmental arm of her Son.) The second distressing theme is one of an idealized woman, eternally young

* *Ibid.*, p. 188.

and beautiful and perfect. It may be a good spiritual exercise to try to think up what our ideal woman would be; but to think up such a fantasy and then give her a name and try to identify her with a historical human being about whom a very few facts are known! This way lies divorcement from reality. As for Christ's being unapproachable because He is God, this is an old, old heresy condemned a long time ago by your Church, which went to a great deal of trouble to establish the belief that Christ was *fully man* as well as being fully God. You say that you accept the biblical statement that there is one God and one Mediator between God and man, the man Christ Jesus; then why do you insist on having a Mediatrix? Don't send me a long answer to this one. You predicted I wouldn't approve of your consecration to Jesus through, with, in, and for Mary, and I don't; but thanks for letting me know about it. I respect you and admire you too much to pooh-pooh your devotion, although I question the wisdom of the form of it. I could subscribe to the whole consecration formula if it were addressed to God through Jesus Christ rather than to Jesus Christ through Mary. I know that what you have undertaken is not easy, and that it must transform your whole life.

The Third Order of St. Francis and the Legion of Mary Auxiliary sounded more acceptable to me, but I don't understand about the specified daily prayers — "including five decades of the Rosary and the *Magnificat*." My impression is that for five consecutive times you say 10 Hail Mary's, an Our Father, a Glory Be to the Father, the Apostles' Creed and the Hail, Holy Queen, adding to these the *Magnificat* daily. Do you do all this kneeling in one place at one time? Do you have a special time each day when you do it? I understand that you also go to Mass every morning. At what time? Wow. Then there's the Office for the Third Order. You have a choice there. What do you choose? If any of these questions are an unwelcome invasion of your devotional privacy, ignore them. But I'd honestly like to know what happens in your mind while you are going through all those repetitions, which I have no right to call vain if they are means of grace to you. Can you meditate fruitfully while saying all those specified words over and over, day after day? I'm not asking whether you have periods of spiritual dryness. I'm sure you must, and in those times you go through the motions and the words without being wholly there yourself. But tell me about the good times, if you feel that you can and want to. Do you schedule any additional time for prayers in your own words, or are these scattered through the day as you go about your work?

In my private devotions I use some of the prayers in our *Prayer Book*, especially those in the "Family Prayer" section (p. 587 ff.), and some of the Sunday Collects. (The one for the Fourth Sunday after Easter, this week's, is one I like: "O Almighty God, who alone canst order the unruly wills and affections of sinful men; Grant unto thy people, that they may love the thing which thou commandest, and desire that which thou dost promise; that so, among the sundry and manifold changes of the world, our hearts may surely there be fixed, where true joys are to be found; through Jesus Christ our Lord. Amen," p. 174.) I tend, however, to use my own words and to try to line up my will with God's will. I haven't a set time or place for daily prayer, and I tend to slide through some days with nothing but the short prayers that are a part of all my life and the "background music" of meditation that occupies my mind whenever I am engaged in a repetitive task that doesn't require thought. I usually go to Communion twice weekly, on Sunday and Wednesday mornings, at 9 o'clock. (I am not a "morning person" and am grateful for these relatively late Communions. I don't go fasting.)

Do you ever practice contemplation? I have tried it on a few occasions and have found it richly rewarding, a unitive experience heightening all my powers in the apprehension of something true and most high. I found familiar symbols realigned and filled full with meaning. I'm a little scared of contemplation and feel it should be practiced under a spiritual director, if at all.

Now let me complain a bit, as I threatened to do in my last letter and you invited me to in your last. Here on a mission field we are often made conscious of the practical irritations in the Protestant-Catholic tension. According to a long-established agreement among the major Protestant denominations, only one of them works in a single mission field so as not to confuse the people with a multiplicity of approaches. Thus, to a very great extent, the Roman Catholic Church and the Protestant Episcopal Church represent Christianity on this Indian reservation. Mormons, Jehovah's Witnesses, and certain Pentecostal sects do not observe the Protestant agreement, but their influence is minor. How I wish sometimes for the benevolent and cooperative proximity of some Methodists and Presbyterians! Instead we have only the two main Churches, and one of them claims insistently that it is the only true Church! The Episcopal Church runs a foster-home program for Indian children. The home admits children referred to it by the tribal social worker, who is a Roman Catholic, and for some reason known only to her the children are mostly Roman Catholics. They attend the parochial school 20 miles away and go to a weekly catechism class at the little church down the road from this mission, where they live. One of the girls who was here last year was constantly telling our oldest daughter that the Episcopal Church was not a true Church, in spite of the obvious fact that the Episcopal Church was feeding her, clothing her, sheltering her, and giving her the love she had failed to get in her Roman Catholic home. I suppose the priest who instructed her felt that he had to warn her against the dangers of being around here, but I object to having our daughter, whom we are trying to bring up as a Christian, told that her parents are all wrong. Another instance: shortly after we arrived at this mission, my husband was called to an Indian house to administer Holy Communion to an elderly woman who was suffering from cancer. On several occasions he took Communion to her, first at her home and later at the hospital, where she went to die. She had been baptized by an Episcopal priest on January 2, 1905, and confirmed by an Episcopal bishop on October 25, 1914, and had continued a communicant of this Church for 46 years, which is a good long time. In the last few days of her life she was not conscious.

When the time for the funeral came, her Roman Catholic family asked their priest to have the service in the Roman Catholic Church. This was their privilege, in the absence of a will or other written directive from the woman who had died. My husband attended the service and heard, to his astonishment, that this woman, shortly before her death, had asked to be baptized in the Roman Catholic faith, and had been so baptized. My husband did not question the fact of her rebaptism (55 years after her baptism in the Name of the Father, and of the Son, and of the Holy Ghost), but he privately questioned her physical ability and her spiritual desire to request it.

Lately I have heard, from one of our young women members, that one of the Jesuit priests who run the Roman Catholic mission to the Indians has been bothering her repeatedly with allegations that she and her husband (a nominal, nonpracticing Roman Catholic whose marriage to her was solemnized in the Episcopal Church) are living in sin and that their children are illegitimate. The probable outcome of this instance of Jesuit zeal will be that the husband will ask to be received into the Episcopal Church.

This reservation has enough real sin and enough genuine spiritual need to take up all the time of all the priests either Church would care to send here. We do not spend our time fighting your Church's representatives on the reservation. We wish they wouldn't waste their time fighting us. Oh, how I hope that 100 years from now both great groups of Christians, Catholic and Protestant, will be together and will be working together in missions, both domestic and foreign!

By now I know the Catholic answers to my Protestant objections on this practical level. I'm just terribly sorry that bad feeling and mistrust are being generated in the name of the Prince of Peace, the King of Love.

Is my husband "High" or "Low" Church? I have a hard time getting answers to questions like that: he is the unwordiest preacher I ever met. From 15 years of observation I'd say he is a "Low" Churchman, but he doesn't work zealously at being one in opposition to the other kinds. Our Bishop is outspokenly "Low" in his churchmanship and expects "Low" Church practices from his clergy. I am about as "Low" as they come; in fact there are times when I tease my husband by saying I am a "confirmed" Presbyterian.

I'd better stop and give you some time for Küng. I hope he'll provide some dialogue matter other than what I've mentioned.

I ran across a quotation in my notebook the other day, and I can't remember where I found it. I usually write down sources, but I have none for this: "What is faith but infinite patience toward God? And what is hope but infinite patience toward oneself? And what is love but infinite patience toward one's neighbor?" A bit passive in tone maybe, but worth meditating. I shall pray for you.

With love,

BETTY

P.S. I'll bite: what's the "J.M.J." at the heading of your letters one and six? We've made a guess.

Yes, Ware's still with us. He claims our letters have "degenerated into an annotated bibliography." Oh, dear.

✝ ✝ ✝ ✝ ✝

CARLSBAD, NEW MEXICO

June 13

Dear Betty,

Forgive me for being so late. One reason is that I have put in more hours at the hospitals the past three weeks. I'm the extra help in the Medical Records Department at each hospital and sometimes neither one needs me; last month was a thin one, as the doctors didn't seem to be in a dictating mood, but they are making up for it now. It's been necessary for me to juggle all my evenings and any extra hours I can squeeze in as well between the two places to keep them both happy. I love the work — I've been doing it so long that the medical terminology, spelling, etc., give me no particular difficulties, and it never gets dull. It's like having dozens of mystery stories going at once. I wonder whether the admitting diagnosis will be confirmed or disproved by the X-ray and laboratory studies, how the patient will react to treatment, what will show up on surgery, and the like. I find the "in-patient" dictation much more interesting than "old" dictation (when the doctor waits until after the patient has left the hospital to dictate the history, physical examination, operative record, etc.) because of that element of suspense. Nurses who enjoy working directly with the patients might find my work tedious, sitting five hours at a stretch with a dictaphone and typewriter, but every man to his own taste. I have the Record Room to myself most of the time, few interruptions and those enjoyable, and it is such a rest from the noisy confusion at home that sometimes I can hardly wait to get there.

I'm fortunate in having part-time work that I enjoy so much and can do at flexible hours. Usually I work from 4 to 9, sometimes I don't go until 5, sometimes I quit at 7 if I have a meeting to attend, once in awhile I put in 3 or 4 hours in the morning, though not often. Joe works shifts and his schedule changes every 8 to 12 days; seven graveyards when he's away from about 9:30 p.m. to 7:30 a.m., two days off, seven afternoons (1:30 to 11:30 p.m.), one off, seven days (5:30 to 3:30) and then four days off. Then back on graveyard again. Some wives dislike shift work but most of us get used to it and look forward to the advantages each change of shift brings and don't find any of them unbearable. In our other house graveyard was particularly difficult because of the noise which kept him from sleeping and had me shushing kids all day until I was ready to scream myself, but it is slightly better since we moved. However, one week of graveyard is plenty, and we've had more than that lately. The hourly workers at the potash mines are on strike; Joe is a salaried worker who still has a job (thank God!) but he is on straight nights without any days off for the duration of the strike, which started June 1.

. . . I am reading Küng with appreciation whenever I can snatch a few moments and am grateful for the opportunity. There is nothing in his discussion as far as I have read that conflicts with my concept of the Catholic Church. I thoroughly agree with his contention concerning the constant necessity for renewal and reformation within the Church itself; this in no way contradicts or invalidates belief in her essential divinity and infallibility. The important thing is to distinguish between what is accidental and what is essential. Many of the incidental aspects of Catholicism could be changed or eliminated; but the essence cannot be tampered with without distorting and emasculating and failing to transmit authentically the truths and means of salvation instituted by Christ.

The Knox book sounds fascinating and I hope to read it when you are finished. I have the highest regard for him as a writer and thinker and theologian. A few years back a priest loaned me *Window in the Wall,* a collection of Corpus Christi sermons on the Holy Eucharist and the Real Presence preached by Monsignor Knox over a period of many years. I raved so much about the book the next time I saw him that he told me I could keep it if I wanted to, but, fool that I was, I returned it when I finished and have been kicking myself for it ever since.

The Huxley book doesn't hold any appeal for me, for reasons similar to those your husband gave initially for being dubious about our dialogue: his presuppositions are so radically different from mine that I find whatever he writes frustrating and exasperating. I wrote to him once about an article he had in *The Saturday Evening Post;* his answer confirmed the fact that when we use the same words we don't mean the same things at all.

Neither am I interested in reading Father Teilhard de Chardin's book because I know it is over my head and I haven't the leisure or uncluttered mind to absorb and comprehend it. It is my understanding that Father Teilhard's superiors refused to give permission to publish *The Phenomenon of Man* not because it was heretical but because it is easily liable to misinterpretation by those untrained in philosophy and theology and hence is dangerous in inexpert hands. I will not judge them. The book is not on the Index, but I think the Holy Office has issued warnings regarding it. Truth "placed side by side with error" will *not* necessarily prevail in individual minds. Ultimately, yes; but the history of mankind should surely make it clear that few men have the keenness of intellect combined with the humility and faith which will enable them always to distinguish between God's truth and the subtle distortions of it planted and fostered by the Father of Liars.

Your question about how a lay person finds out what is on the Index is one I can't answer. My edition of the *Catholic Almanac* (1958) states that the last edition of the Index was published in 1948 and that prohibitions since that time have been published in *Acta Apostolicae Sedis*, the official publication of the Holy See. I have never seen a list of the forbidden books myself. You remember I mentioned that I had dropped a note to Father Klister inquiring about some of the books you discussed? He wrote back that he had not been able to find anything on any of them except a biographical piece in the *Encyclopaedia Britannica* on von Hügel, which he had copied for me. "The general law of the Church forbids us to read those books which are injurious to faith," he wrote. "I am unable to judge whether any of these are of this classification, not having read them. However, I would presume that your faith is strong enough and that you would not be perverted by them, and your conscience should be your guide. If you have further doubts, show them to a local priest and ask his opinion."

I am afraid the Brunner book would come under the classification of being potentially "injurious to faith." The divine authority of the Church is at the very foundation of my faith; the assumption that Christ did not found a Church with the authority to teach His truths without error but left men to scramble around making up their own theories as to what He really meant when He said this or that — blind men following the blind — does not strike me as being reasonable from the point of view of either God or man. The Catholic faith is a supernatural gift; it is not contrary to reason but it can be weakened or killed by being unnecessarily exposed to arguments against it. The Catholic who loses his faith in his Church has only two directions to go — down or out. He becomes an agnostic, doubting everything and finding no peace of mind anywhere, or he "joins" a Church which teaches without any claim to infallibility but which is thus "easier" because it can change its doctrines with the prevailing winds and tell him he is now free to do things he was previously taught were serious sins.

I am afraid somebody is misrepresenting the Catholic teaching regarding the legitimacy of children of couples whose marriages are civilly legal but invalid under the laws of the Catholic Church. *Radio Replies* says that if the marriage is legal according to civil law, the children are legitimate according to that law. Are the children illegitimate in Catholic law? It depends. "If both or either of the parties thought they were contracting a valid marriage the children are legitimate. . . . Catholic law declares that the children of a marriage invalid in itself, yet in which one of the parties at least is in good faith, are to be held as legitimate."*

Only God can judge whether the "nominal, nonpracticing Roman Catholic" husband was aware of the gravity of his failure to comply with the laws of his Church when he contracted marriage in a Protestant Church. Marriage is a sacrament, and the Church has the right to make rules safeguarding and regulating the reception of it for her people. Objectively, he is living in sin and cannot receive the sacraments of penance or Holy Eucharist as long as he remains in a union unrecognized by her. I can't find anything on it right now, but I know that persons born out of wedlock cannot become priests or religious without obtaining a special dispensation: illegitimacy is an impediment to a religious vocation, principally because of the danger of scandal. If children of invalidly married Catholics are canonically invalid in the eyes of the Church, I presume the impediment would exist for them too.

Your views on baptism were evidently shared by the early Church. St. Augustine relates that when he was still a child, he fell gravely ill and begged for baptism but when he suddenly recovered, the "baptismal cleansing" was postponed,

> for it was argued that if I lived I should inevitably fall again into the filth of sin: and after baptism the guilt of sin's defile-

* *Radio Replies,* Vol. I, No. 1288.

> ment would be in itself graver and put the soul in graver peril. . . . I ask You, my God . . . to what end was my baptism deferred? Was it for my good that I was left to sin with a loose rein, or was the rein not truly loosed? Why do we constantly hear such phrases as: "Let him alone, let him keep on with what he is doing, he is not yet baptized"? In the matter of the body's health we do not say: "Let him be wounded worse, he is not yet cured." It would have been far better had I been made whole at once and had so used my own efforts and the aid of my friends that the health brought to my soul should be safe in Your keeping, by whose gift it was given me. Far better, I say.*

Obviously, the custom changed as time went on, probably because of a clearer theological understanding of the nature and effects of baptism. (Sometimes, I will admit, I look at my children and wonder what good the sacrament did them! — But how do I know they would not have been worse without it?)

I do not object to answering your questions about how I pray but am afraid you may find my answer unexciting. My alarm is set for 6 in the morning, but I usually start waking up around 5, and — this is a grace, I know, not something due to a conscious effort on my part — my first thoughts are generally "acts of love" (a Catholic expression meaning expressions of love) directed to God. In this nice, drowsy, half-awake state, I just love God and feel grateful to Him for loving me, with occasional aspirations running through my mind, like: "Oh, Jesus, I love You" or "O Lord, our Lord, how wonderful is Thy name in all the earth" . . . "I'm all Yours and all that I have is Yours" . . . and similar ejaculations and bits of psalms or hymns that well up spontaneously in between catnaps. When I am sufficiently wide awake, without getting out of bed, I generally make the Morning Offering of all my thoughts, words, and actions of the day, using a formula I know by heart.

I get dressed, put the coffee pot on, and drive or walk the three blocks to the church for 6:30 Mass. I keep the Legion of Mary leaflet in my missal and read the obligatory prayers

---

* *Confessions*, Book One, F. J. Sheed tr. © 1943 Sheed & Ward, Inc., New York.

(which include versicles, antiphons, three prayers from the missal, one of them your Whitsunday Collect, and a long prayer for the Legion and its members, together with the *Magnificat*) before or during the first few minutes of Mass, omitting the Rosary at that time. I always receive Holy Communion.

The next time I formally pray (excepting grace at meals) is right after lunch when I lie down with the children for a nap and, using rosary beads to keep track of the number, start silently praying the Franciscan office of 12 Our Fathers, 12 Hail Marys, and 12 Glorys. There is a meditation connected with the Passion for each Our Father-Hail Mary-Glory which I sometimes try to think about. Much of the time, I'm afraid, the Office is more or less an *obbligato* on one level of my mind while my thoughts dart here and there on another level; but my intentions are united with God even if my attention is flighty. I usually doze off before I finish but my fingers hold the bead I was on and I complete the Office when I wake up in 15 or 20 minutes, before getting up.

My daily Rosary comes at bedtime. Sometimes I read too long and am too sleepy to meditate; at such times the Rosary is more a penance, an effort of the will, than prayer per se. Penances are prayers, too, and sometimes vice versa. But most nights the Rosary is for me a gathering together of all the day has brought and a contemplating of first one aspect, then another, with Jesus and Mary. The Our Fathers and Hail Marys are again the silent vocal *obbligato;* the physical "running" of the beads provides the bodily participation and an anchor to prevent complete distraction; the Mysteries are the springboards to mental prayer. I will enclose a little booklet that may help you understand how the Rosary can be far more than a "vain repetition" of vocal prayers; I would like it back as I don't have another copy. I don't often use the book itself while I am praying the Rosary but in times of dryness it helps.

Actually, I'm not much for reading prayers out of books, although I have managed to accumulate quite an assortment of prayer books and many of the thoughts expressed in the prayers are well conceived and beautifully articulated. A Minnesota reader last week sent me this quotation from one of the Trappist Father Raymond's books:

> Hence I must tell you now that a prayerful man is a man who always prays, but not one who is always saying prayers. A life of prayer is not a life spent on one's knees, incessantly talking to God; it is a life wherein man is ever conscious of the God within him and without him, above him and below him, over, under, and all around him. To be a man of prayer, then, is to be a man whose every thought, word, and deed is not about God, but directed to God; a man who eats and drinks, sleeps and works, laughs and cries, suffers and rejoices, triumphs and fails in God and for God's honor and glory.*

And while we're on the subject of prayer, the "J.M.J." at the heading of some of the letters simply means that I consciously remembered to say a prayer for guidance before I began writing. Haven't you ever watched Bishop Sheen on TV? He puts it at the top of his blackboard, and my children learn from Sister to put it on their school papers. I know the letters stand for Jesus, Mary, and Joseph, but I do not know whether others use a prayer formula each time. I don't—with me, it just means something like: "Jesus, Mary, Joseph, help me see the truth clearly and express it simply, for the glory of God and the salvation of souls; don't let me write anything that will hurt or mislead whoever may read it."

I am very much interested in contemplation, though apparently we do not have quite the same understanding of the meaning of the term. Catholic mystical writers distinguish between two kinds of contemplation, "acquired" and "infused." The first is capable of being attained with one's own efforts and the ordinary grace of God; the second "is a free gift bestowed by God when and on whom He pleases" (Tanquerey); it is not something we can acquire ourselves by practicing. I have some very interesting books on the subject of the higher stages of prayer which I will be happy to send you whenever you want to read them, particularly St. Teresa's *Interior Castle* and Thomas Verner Moore's *The Life of Man With God*. You would also enjoy Thomas

* Father Raymond, O.C.S.O., *Burnt Out Incense* (New York: P. J. Kenedy & Sons, 1949), p. xv.

Merton's *The Sign of Jonas* and at least portions of his *Ascent to Truth*. I know you would like Tanquerey's *Spiritual Life* but hesitate to offer to send it because it isn't a book you can skim hurriedly and I am reluctant to part with it even for a week.

I long for contemplation but apparently it is not God's will for me at this time. Quite a few years ago, before the last four babies began arriving, I used to make an early morning hour of meditation before the Blessed Sacrament daily, and even after I was unable to do that I made at least one hour of adoration in church each week, usually on Sunday afternoon. At that time I think I had the "prayer of quiet" fairly often. Bob was the one who used to watch the kids while I went, but in the past two or three years he was busy working and dating and then he got married and left. Neither my husband nor the next two boys are in sympathy with my running away from my family and housework to kneel in church, so I gave up the holy hours, but not daily Mass. In the past year or two I have had only very rare touches of what might be infused prayer. Tanquerey states that "God is wont to adapt His graces (of prayer) to the temperament and duties of state of each individual," and he notes also that "Contemplation is not sanctity, but only one of the most effective means of attaining it."* I do not feel that God has deserted me nor I Him; I might use the analogy of a married couple who are unable to express their love physically because of the constant presence of relatives in the house; their love for each other is not diminished and is revealed in little glances and smiles, and the eventual union may be all the sweeter because of the delay.

I made some notes on *Answer Me This* but don't think I'll enumerate them. The thing I noted most about the book was the lack of authority: so many questions were sidestepped or answered with personal opinions, and it seemed to me there were inconsistencies in the appeals to authoritative sources (i.e., Bible, early Councils, Articles of Religion, etc.) for what was answered positively.

I'm sorry as can be that this letter is so late — I'm afraid it

* Tanquerey, *The Spiritual Life*, p. 733.

can't possibly get there before you leave on vacation and hope you've made arrangements to have your mail forwarded.

With love,

LORRAINE

✝ ✝ ✝ ✝ ✝

ETHETE, WYOMING
July 16

Dear Lorraine,

Your prayer life may not be exciting, but it is impressive. After I wrote you about mine, I decided I was not spending enough time each day in formal prayer; but I haven't changed my practice noticeably. Occasionally I slip next door to the church and spend a quiet time reading Morning or Evening Prayer with the lessons for the day and addressing my own prayers to God, mostly prayers of adoration and intercession. Whenever I have to wait for somebody else (and this is rather often), I spend the time in prayer. Otherwise my daily prayer is a moment-to-moment thing, living in God's presence and referring to Him the events of the day as they come along.

I tried repeating the Lord's Prayer several times, but I didn't like doing it. In moments of solitude the most meaningful words of others to me are the words of hymns. I know three or four stanzas of a great many hymns by heart, and I sing them whenever I drive the car alone any distance. Once last summer I arrived quite hoarse at a meeting in Casper, 150 miles away! While I was reading your books about the Curé d'Ars and St. Francis and your book by Father Faber, I kept singing hymns appropriate to the books. For the Curé, I sang "Christian, Dost Thou See Them" (556). Of course St. Francis rated his own hymn, which in our hymnal begins "Most High, Omnipotent, Good Lord" (307); and while reading Father Faber's essays I began humming, "There's a Wideness in God's Mercy" (304) without realizing that he himself had written the words.

. . . The nun's autobiography you sent me and the lives of the two saints (Vianney and Francis) all left me wondering how a good Catholic draws the line between Christian asceticism and neurotic masochism. I believe in self-discipline and in being willing and able to endure hardship for the sake of Jesus Christ; but scourging oneself in the name of Christ? No. Wearing an iron chain until it becomes embedded in the flesh? No.

You find an Anglican question-and-answer book lacking in authority; I find the Catholic *Radio Replies* replete with an authority I can't accept. (I haven't done any underlining or marginal commenting in these three volumes because your children use them as school references, and my comments would have been in the nature of refutation and often in the tone of indignation.) The replies to crank-type questions were sound and reasonable and admirably calm, but the misconceptions about Protestantism that your priest-answerers show are most annoying. Here again we come to the hard, solid rock of the wall that separates us: it is in the very nature of your Church to insist that she alone is It and has The Answers. Now I see that, according to your Church's teaching, it really is your duty to pray for my conversion. Also, the more my ignorance about your Church is dispelled, the more danger I am in, according to the Catholic viewpoint. As long as I was just a poor ignorant Protestant stumbling around without any real knowledge of your truth, but living as a Christian according to the best knowledge I had, your Church would admit that I had a chance of salvation by the mercy of God. Now, as I understand the Catholic position, as soon as my ignorance of your faith is overcome, I am in mortal danger if I still reject your Church's claims.

Such reasoning might have prevailed with me, and certainly would have put a shadow of fear into my heart, 20 years ago when I was a Fundamentalist. I suppose the reason that rabid Protestant anti-Catholics are likely to be Fundamentalists is that the two groups have so much in common. For both Fundamentalists and Roman Catholics, believing the right set of creedal statements is necessary for salvation. The more prevalent Protestant viewpoint is that creeds are very helpful in expressing Christian thought about the God to whom they point, but they are not to be used as a test of "right belief," that right belief is an active trust in a Person, not an intellectual assent to certain statements about that Person.

As a Fundamentalist I accepted a supreme authority, the authority of the Bible, just as you accept a supreme authority, the authority of your Church. I still cherish the Bible and live by it as the primary source of knowledge about the Lord Jesus Christ; but my faith is in the living Lord, not in the words of Scripture themselves. You see, my whole attitude has changed around. Whereas before I probably would have been harshly intolerant of Catholics if there had been many around (they were an insignificant minority where I grew up), I had a set of mind that might have been conducive to conversion toward Catholicism. Now I feel free to love and appreciate my Catholic friends and their Church without having the slightest inclination to become a part of that Church.

Whereas before every aspect of belief had its tight little pigeonhole, now I find large gaps in the intellectual framework that surrounds the central affirmation of my life, "I believe in the Lord Jesus Christ." I expect to fill in the gaps as I grow in knowledge and wisdom, but I do not fret about their existence. This sort of Protestant attitude, I know, leads you and other writers to speak of us as stumbling around in the dark, being blind leaders of the blind. The Protestants I know who are committed Christians are far from being a stumbling lot: they are characterized by their freedom, their love, their peace, their joy. They don't know all the answers, and they don't expect their Churches to have all the answers, but they walk in faith, and they believe that God walks with them.

I've wondered, too, whether you and I think alike on many issues because of our common Presbyterian heritage. I wonder whether you're glad you have that background to your Catholicism? Probably that's a "rotten-egg" question. (Our vacation trip to Minnesota, 1000 miles away, was made much more endurable by our ruling that anyone who asked, "How much farther is it?" or "How long will it take to get there?" was a rotten egg. Since then we've found it handy in other situations to be able to say, "That's a rotten-egg question.") I feel that I'm a much better Episcopalian for having been a Presbyterian. The Episcopal Church is satisfyingly complete in its worship, but it is too "Catholic" for me in two respects — the lack of emphasis on individual acquaintance with the Bible, and the lack of any stress on a personal conversion experience. The thorough knowledge of the Bible and the deep sense of personal commitment which I received as a Presbyterian have fit in well with being an Episcopalian, but I am not sure I should have had these bonuses if I had been brought up in the Episcopal Church. I do believe it would be helpful for every adult Protestant Church member to examine his faith and his Church affiliation and find out whether he ought to switch to another denomination than the one in which he grew up. Many would find themselves most at home where they are, but many others would discover that they were more suited by temperament and grown-up belief to a different Church environment. Of course your own situation is quite different: you've found what you think is the only true Church. I suppose you must wish you had been in it from infancy. But hasn't your Presbyterian background enhanced in some ways your appreciation of Catholicism? We differ drastically, but we differ as *Christians*. It was as a Christian that you were a Presbyterian; it is as a Christian that you are a Catholic.

My questions about confirmation in my last letter were aimed at my attempt to understand whether there is some definitive experience within the Catholic framework which can be called an experience of personal commitment to Christianity. Some of our Episcopalian priests use preparation for confirmation partly as preparation for the individual person's acceptance of the Lord Jesus Christ for himself; others prepare the confirmands without any such emphasis on personal decision. I feel that in practice it is possible to be a Catholic or an Episcopalian without being a Christian, and I feel that the existence of prominent Catholics and Episcopalians who are not Christians can deter our respective churches as they seek to give a Christian witness to the rest of the world. (In theory, of course, all Catholics and all Episcopalians are Christians. It's the practice I'm talking about.)

Every time I come up hard against the stone wall of your Church's claim to supernatural freedom from error, I get discouraged and wonder what's the sense of going on with our conversation; but I like conversing with you, and I feel we have yet to explore several explorable paths. Let's continue: shall we?

In one of your columns you mention AA meetings. I've never been to one, but I have drunk a lot of coffee with members after their meetings. (Alcoholics seem to be awfully intemperate about coffee, but caffeine is a lot better than alcohol for them.) Ware has been to numbers of AA meetings and to conferences on alcoholism, and he has been asked to speak to local AA groups. (He can't begin his talk by saying, "My name is Ware, and I am an alcoholic," because he isn't; he says, "My name is Ware, and I am a sinner.") My sense of stewardship of body, mind, and will enters into my own attitude toward drinking. (I have very few inhibitions, but I place a high value on the ones I have.) As an Episcopalian I've had to become accustomed to seeing priests and faithful church members take a relaxing drink or two on social occasions. Ware and I have both found it difficult to cultivate the art of being unself-consciously pleasant while sitting in a bar sipping ginger ale while most of the others were sipping stronger stuff. I do what I can to encourage hostesses to serve nonalcoholic drinks on the same tray with alcoholic ones, to give their guests freedom of choice with no social pressures. I admire the gracious way one hostess handled the pre-luncheon drink situation at a small party I went to not long ago. Instead of asking everybody to state a preference, she brought in a tray containing glasses of sherry and glasses of tomato juice, more glasses than there were guests. Thus each could take what she wanted without any embarrassment.

Drinking problems are severe here on the Indian reservation. Social drinking for relaxation is not the custom; one drinks to get drunk. Alcoholics Anonymous in its usual form seems to have little appeal except to a few Indians who feel at home in a predominantly non-Indian group. Our State Hospital has had encouraging success with intensive group therapy for alcoholics. I'd like to see what it could do with an all-Indian group, but it would be hard to get such a group together. The social and economic pressures for staying sober that operate in the white community barely exist here, where almost nobody has a steady job and a man's parents and wife are as likely to get drunk as he is. The Church's main specific deterrent to alcoholism here is the pledge, which numbers of Indian men and women take on their own initiative before God's altar, promising to abstain from alcoholic beverages for a period of time which they specify. (Nobody yet has taken a pledge for the AA's specified 24 hours at a time, which might be more realistic; the time may be as short as one month or as long as five years or as realistic as "until December 24.") In Indian thinking this type of religious pledge has a binding force. A person can say, "I've taken a pledge," and the one who is pestering him to come on and go to town and have a few drinks will often respect the other's vow and leave him alone. (The same Jesuit who tells couples of mixed religion that their children are illegitimate also tells Indians that their pledges in the Episcopal Church are not valid before God. The Indians who take the pledges believe they are valid and find help and strength in them.)

I think Alcoholics Anonymous is a tremendous force for good in any community. I haven't had any contact with Al-Anon or Ala-Teen, which help the families of alcoholics live with their problems; but I think the whole movement can provide a wholesome example to the Church. Surely the fellowship which alcoholics and their families find in these groups is kin to the fellowship Christians should be able to find in their Churches. Aren't Churches, after all, a kind of "Sinners Anonymous," except that the names of the sinners are known and dear to God?

Before we moved to the reservation, where snobbery isn't much of a factor, I used to be alarmed at Church members' expressions of satisfaction at "what a nice class of people we have here at St. Swithin's" and at the consternation some women showed when a "different" sort of person showed up at a meeting of the guild. In all kinds of Christian Churches I get the impression that "fellowship" is a pretty superficial thing; yet in every Church I've ever visited were some individuals with whom I could find true fellowship, which is based on a common faith in the Lord Jesus Christ rather than on certain social similarities. Even in meetings of clergy wives the superficial type of fellowship is evident when some of the wives gang up and talk about the one who smokes cigarillos, wears astonishing color combinations, and displays a certain lack of social know-how. Yet I've found true fellowship with the woman who has these odd habits: she also has the habit of belief, the habit of commitment, in her own way, to God. Age, social class, economic status, skin color, and personal eccentricities all become unimportant when one is in love with God and in love and charity with other persons. The fellowship you and I have together in Christ even cuts across some creedal lines which are very important to you.

I'm going to have to quit now, for this is a wild week. We're all sewing on name tapes like mad for the three girls, who are going away Saturday for a month at camp. I have to collect 12 usable sheets and nine blankets and then hope there'll be something unragged to put on the beds for all the guests we're expecting. There's a potluck supper at one of our churches tonight, and sometime tomorrow seven of Ware's cousins will descend on us. I haven't met them, and he hasn't seen any of them for more than 15 years, during which time most of them were born. Things will be a little busy entertaining them and getting the three girls off to camp on the train, which is 50 miles from here. (The camp wants us to check their baggage a day early, but I don't think we'll be driving the extra 100 miles.) Then Sunday a very *neat* family of four will arrive to visit the reservation, and see the last of the Arapaho Sun Dance, which begins tomorrow night. The neat family may or may not stay with us, but either way I'll have to try to be neat too, although the only towels the girls will leave will be utterly disreputable.

You'd better not send me any books that require thought for a while. Several copies of the *Register* came today, and I'm enjoying them (between name tapes and laundry loads). Do you want them back? I am especially delighted with your sentiments on funerals.

It is going to be very strange for the next month to have one child only, but we can take it. I meant to tell you in this letter how we feel about birth control, which we practice conscientiously; but I'd better wait until another time.

Love,

BETTY

⸻

CARLSBAD, NEW MEXICO
August 23

Dear Betty,

Your comparison of the similar "set of mind" of Fundamentalist Protestants and Catholics was thoughtful and extremely interesting, as was also your analysis of your present position. I think the latter could bear a little modification. You say that according to your understanding of the Catholic position, when your ignorance of our faith is overcome you are in mortal danger if you reject our Church's claims. But it is not merely knowledge of the Church's teachings that is required, but faith in them — acceptance of their truth — that is required for conversion.

A person who refuses to study the "credentials" of the Church for fear he may be convinced of their truth is not acting in good faith and may be in a dangerous position. A person who believes (even against his will) that the Catholic Church is what she claims but stays out of her fold because he puts personal convenience or material gain or the opinion of others, et cetera, ahead of his inner convictions is acting contrary to his own conscience and is not in a very safe position. But if a person is given the opportunity to study Catholic teachings and does and through no fault of his own is unable to believe them, he is not lost (though he may miss many extra blessings he could have received). Thus as long as you haven't the slightest inclination to become a part of our Church the Holy Spirit has evidently not called you to it.

I know there are millions of wonderful Protestant Christians walking in faith, as you say, not concerned by the fact that their churches acknowledge that they don't have all the answers. Of course God is with them! But some of them do, through a special grace, receive the invitation: "Friend, come up higher." For others the problem never arises.

At any rate, as long as you are absolutely honest with yourself and with God and willing to follow wherever He wills to lead you, I am sure you will be all right.

Yes, I would certainly agree that my Presbyterian background has enhanced my appreciation of Catholicism, although not necessarily in exactly the way you mean. I can't remember if I've spoken before of a simile that seems to me to describe the relationship of the different Churches and the portions of Truth they possess. Imagine it all as a beautiful, perfect picture, created by God, but cut up in pieces like a jigsaw puzzle. Right in the center of the picture is Christ. All of the Christian Churches have this central part of the picture, but from there on, no two denominations or sects have exactly the same pieces: one has mainly pieces in this corner, one in that, with considerable overlapping, of course. Only the Catholic Church has all the pieces, and thus she is the only one with the full picture. Of course all analogies limp and can't be carried too far, but this one will bear a little more thought. Because the Calvinistic Churches, for instance, have a preponderance of pieces concerning predestination, as compared with some of the other doctrines, they have tended to focus on them and assume for them a significance unjustified in relation to the picture as a whole. Each Church sees her own portion of the picture more clearly than she can see that which the other Churches have. And, lacking some of the pieces into which the ones she has should fit, she is apt to turn some of the latter the wrong way.

Because of this intense focusing on particular aspects of Christianity while neglecting others, it is possible that in practice some sects actually have brighter, clearer colors in certain portions of their pictures than does the Catholic Church herself (i.e., popular familiarity with the Bible) — but the Catholic Church has the only truly balanced and complete picture, even though some of her pieces are not as clearly defined as they ultimately will be.

Because of my early Sunday School and Vacation Bible School training I am more familiar with some of the Bible than many of my born-Catholic friends (though there are other parts, such as the first chapter of St. Luke's Gospel, which are far more familiar to Catholics than to Protestants). I have a better understanding of Catholic theology than some born-Catholics do because of having been introduced to it as an adult: I studied the reason and the logic behind many of the things they take for granted simply because they grew up believing them. These are two advantages of having come into the Catholic Church as an adult and of my own free will. On the other hand, I think I would have made some different decisions in my youth had I had the advantage of early Catholic training — perhaps not, but I think I would have.

The austerities and self-imposed penances you found so distasteful in your Catholic reading are not necessarily to be imitated; in fact, as a rule the Church strongly discourages extraordinary bodily mortifications such as those you describe. She even more strongly, however, insists that some penance is not only desirable but absolutely essential, and in this she is only passing on what she has received: "Unless you do penance you shall all likewise perish" . . . "If anyone will come after Me, let him take up his cross, *deny himself* and follow Me." Penance is necessary: (1) to discipline our bodies and strengthen our wills to enable them to choose what is right and forgo what is evil and (2) to make reparation for our past sins and the negligences and sins of others and thus "fill up what is lacking" in the Mystical Body of Christ. The person whose gluttony has fattened him must go to the other extreme in order to regain his proper weight — he must diet strictly, taking less than he needs until the proper balance is restored. The one who has sinned seriously and then comes to love God and realize the heinousness of his sins in the light of the infinite mercy and goodness of God may sometimes seem to go to extremes in being harsh with himself, but the same principle is involved.

I know you are acquainted with St. Paul's doctrine of the Mystical Body: we are all members of one body, with Christ the Head. If one member of a body hurts, the whole body is handicapped: if your head aches, you can't do your work as well as usual, if you cut off a toe the others have to work extra hard to maintain your balance in walking, etc. Weak and sinful members hurt the whole Mystical Body, but fervent Christians can counteract their effect and help make reparation for them by extra self-denial, mortification, and penance. The Church teaches that ordinarily it is better to accept the trials God sends than to choose our own; but there are extraordinary persons like the Curé of Ars, with his cold potatoes and nightly disciplines, who are given the grace to do much more — and can't you judge by their fruits that God accepted their sacrifices and found them pleasing in His sight?

I'm sorry I overlooked answering your question regarding confirmation. In the Catholic Church, confirmation is a sacrament by which we receive a special strengthening grace designed to help us profess our faith openly and defend it against those who would attack it. The catechism says the sacraments always give grace to those who receive them with the right dispositions, and that to receive confirmation properly it is necessary to be in the state of grace and to know well the chief truths and duties of our religion. You ask if there is some definitive experience within the Catholic framework which can be called "an experience of personal commitment to Christianity" and say that some Episcopalian priests use preparation for confirmation partly as such a preparation for the individual's acceptance of Christ. I do not know that priests emphasize that angle, although I cannot imagine that the Church would object to a priest's endeavor to encourage such a disposition in those he is preparing for confirmation. The emphasis, however, is on what is received — i.e., the Holy Spirit with His special graces. In practice I must admit that often no change at all can be seen in a person after confirmation; perhaps this is because insufficient attention is given to the aspect of personal consecration.

You keep bringing up the Jesuit who goes around telling your Indians things any instructed Catholic knows are not so. The only explanation that occurs to me is that the story gets twisted by the time it gets to you, either innocently or with malice. Jesuits are probably the most highly educated religious order in the Church — it takes something like 15 years to become a Jesuit priest, compared to maybe six for some of the other orders, and they screen their applicants with the greatest care and weed them out as carefully. There are and have been "bad priests" in the history of the Church who fall away from their vows and then deliberately try to discredit the Catholic Church by lying about her. There are other priests who have let the spirit of the world dull the fervor of their zeal and have perhaps failed to keep as intellectually alert as one would desire, but not, I feel sure, to the point of misrepresenting Catholic moral theology as you have been led to believe this Jesuit does. Did you ever ask him personally about any of the matters you've mentioned? You might be in for a surprise.

A pledge to God, according to my understanding of it, especially one taken at the altar as you describe, would be exactly as "valid" as the individual intends. Your terminology confuses me a bit — I'm not quite sure what you (or he) mean by "valid before God." But any sincere promise or pledge or vow made voluntarily and in good faith by an individual to God would seem to me to be acceptable in the sight of God and binding in conscience on the individual, who could also subsequently expect extra grace from God to enable him to keep the pledge as long as he himself did the best he could. The moral theologian distinguishes between solemn vows which bind under mortal sin and simple vows which bind under venial sin and promises (like the Third Order profession promises) which do not bind under sin: failing to keep the promise is not *ipso facto* a sin. One is never obliged to keep a promise he should not have made in the first place, i.e., to do something wrong; in such case the evil would not be in breaking the promise but in making it in the first place. That is my idea of a promise that is not valid, but that certainly would not apply to the abstinence pledge the Indians take. You say the Indians find help and strength in the pledges and I say God bless 'em!

I've so enjoyed the pictures of your family. Now Ware and Sarah and Martha and Ann and David are more than just names to me. They look like such nice people — I wish you all lived next door. I'm also very pleased with the shots of you — you're much more attractive than in the newspaper photo you sent earlier. I'm afraid I'm vain too: I take a horrible picture and can't believe I'm really that ugly; that's why I didn't send you any group pictures with me in them. The one that goes with the column was taken exactly three years ago in a maternity dress (two months before Betty was born).

If I write any more I'll have to wait until tomorrow as it's time to get ready for work, so I'm going to stop right now and try to get this out before the mailman gets here. If I've left anything unanswered, ask me again, will you? I feel as if my brain has taken a vacation all summer. I hope it comes back home and starts clicking soon.

Love,

LORRAINE

✓ ✓ ✓ ✓ ✓

ETHETE, WYOMING
September 2

Dear Lorraine,

Wherever has the summer gone? Part of ours has been scattered over the American Northwest, and, as we have traveled, I have brought to some of our new experiences the understandings and questions that have been coming out of our dialogue.

In past years I never would have characterized myself as anti-Catholic, but I find now that I have a different, more accepting attitude toward the priests, the nuns, and the Roman Catholic buildings that I see. Although I don't like the statues in the churches, I can understand now that Roman Catholics' use of statues is not necessarily idolatrous. (I wonder whether your grouping together what we consider the first two of the Ten Commandments can have dulled your sensitivity to the dangers of graven images; and whether our grouping together what you consider the last two can have dulled our sensitivity to the sacredness of marriage? By "you" of course I mean Roman Catholics and by "we," Protestants. When you — and in this particular instance the "you" also refers to Lutherans — treat "Thou shalt not covet thy neighbor's wife" as a separate Commandment, you reinforce a point that especially needs to be made these days. We may be vitiating the force of the Commandment by throwing in the house and the servants and the ox and the ass. I do wish we could all get together, all of us Christians that is, on numbering these Commandments and on numbering the Psalms too. Apparently for no very good reason "you" have thrown together Psalms 9 and 10 as they appeared in the Hebrew Psalter, done the same to Hebrew Psalms 114 and 115, divided Hebrew 116 into two psalms, put together your 146 with Hebrew 147, and joined the rest of us with 148. This treasury of Hebrew-Christian poetry which belongs to us all ought not to be a subject of confusion. I had assumed that everyone would know, when someone referred to the Twenty-Third Psalm, that it was the Shepherd Psalm. Nope; for you, that is the Twenty-Second. These are small matters; I hope our churches can smooth out their communications by either agreeing on the same numbering or using a binomial system understandable to both.)

While we were on the West Coast, we had a pleasant visit with an Episcopal priest whose ideas of church ceremonial are far different from ours. He showed us his new Sanctus bell, which he had had imported from England because all he could find in this country were Roman Catholic type with a tinkly sound and he wanted a mellow bong. He mentioned his plans for a rood screen and for statues of SS. John and Mary in the church. As recently as a year ago these preoccupations of his would have alienated me. Now I consider them much less important than his obvious Christian devotion and his appreciation of and pastoral commitment to his parishioners. We were able to enjoy good fellowship with him and his family and to find ourselves united by more than what separates us. He had just returned from a vacation in which he had held services for a month in another parish and was full of the experience he had found there. A goodly number of the men and women there had felt the direct experience of the Holy Spirit during the past year and were sharing in a rich Christian fellowship that was beyond anything this minister had known in ten years in the priesthood. Speaking in tongues was one of the phenomena they had known, but more important was the outgoing concern for their fellow Christians which they showed in many practical ways. Their rector, who had been inclined toward skepticism when he heard reports of similar experiences in other churches, had himself received a "clap-of-thunder"-type visitation which had changed the direction of his life and had found himself an instrument of similar experiences in personal counseling sessions with individual parishioners, who had remained unknown to each other until the rector called them together one day to help him as the instrument of healing a demon-possessed woman. She is now whole, and other members of the parish have continued to enter a deeper fellowship in the Holy Spirit. The man who was telling us about that parish had not received the experience, but he was convinced of its reality in the lives of those who had. He emphasized that these Spirit-filled Episcopalians have, if anything, increased in their loyalty to the services of the Church, receiving Holy Communion frequently, and are not at all inclined to act superior to those members of the parish who have not had the same kind of experience.

When I am deeply moved by what someone has said, I sometimes have a regrettable tendency to "cover up" by being facetious, and I commented to our host, "You know, this sounds like a dangerous thing: making Christians out of the Episcopalians." (I am upset when I realize that a high percentage of my fellow Church members would identify themselves more quickly as Episcopalians than as Christians. Our Church has the Christian faith in such wholeness and richness that I feel very strongly the tragedy of uncommitted lives within its membership.)

The priest laughed and added, "Yes; it scares the hell out of me." He wasn't cursing either.

While we were in Seattle, we attended a three-evening symposium at the World's Fair Playhouse on "Space Age Christianity." It was sponsored by the Episcopal Laymen of the Diocese of Olympia and presented some excellent speakers and some thoughtful and lively discussion. I kept thinking of our dialogue in relation to what was being said, and I'd like to share a few of my thoughts and impressions.

I have gotten the feeling from several of your comments that Catholics suspect Protestants of holding certain views just to be contrary or to express opposition to the Roman Catholic Church. As I observe assemblies such as the one in Seattle and as I read about Roman Catholic and Protestant meetings elsewhere, I am struck with the extent to which Catholics and Protestants ignore each other as significant forces in today's world. A dedicated Catholic attending the Seattle symposium would have found numbers of statements difficult to take, but he would not have found his own Church mentioned or seriously considered. My own impression is that both groups are so wrapped up in their own concerns (often the concerns they believe they share with God) that they are not even aware of the existence of the "other side" of Christendom.

I feel that nothing but good can come out of the presence of numbers of leading Protestants as observers at the Ecumenical Council in Rome. It is high time we all began at least listening to each other — as some leading Catholics politely listened at the last World Council of Churches meeting in New Delhi —

to find out where we really are. I have learned a great deal by listening to you; even where our disagreements are profoundest, I respect your Church profoundly because of the manner in which you have presented its viewpoints.

The moderator of the symposium in Seattle was an internationally known bishop. The six panel members included two clergymen, two medical doctors, a nuclear physicist, a university president, an aircraft company official, and two professors (obviously some of the men "wore two hats"). The variety of opinions presented during the three evenings would have dismayed a Roman Catholic assemblage and confirmed your darkest fears about Protestants' anarchical miscellany of belief. The priest-physicist was orthodox enough both scientifically and religiously, but one of the medical men threw a monkey wrench into the train of thought by admitting Unitarian leanings and disavowing belief in personal survival after death. The discussion ranged widely, and I was impressed by the catholicity of subject matter and of writers who were quoted. St. Augustine, St. Thomas Aquinas, and Pierre Teilhard de Chardin were all mentioned, but the Roman Catholic Church was not. (One speaker cited Thomas Aquinas as having built an admirable bridge between the thought of his century and Christian theology but noted that the bridge had not sufficed to hold up Galileo when he came along.) Another spoke of the need for some means of population control other than war, famine, and disease —and abstinence, added the theologian wit of the group. We were not able to attend the mass worship service (by mass I mean here lots of people, not a form of service) which brought together the discussions into a central focus before God. Perhaps the bishop who spoke was able to summarize all that had been said; perhaps he didn't try. We left the series of discussions feeling that they had been good ventilators of thought but not coherently helpful in relating Christianity to the Space Age. We need more minds working on the relevance of the Gospel to today's peculiar problems.

We enjoyed the meeting and clash of minds, and I couldn't help thinking that such a program would be impossible among

Roman Catholics, who would not tolerate freewheeling and sometimes heretical ideas in an atmosphere of open-minded discussion. I have been thinking in the past several months of the intellectual differences between us — both between you and me and between Roman Catholics and Protestants in general. I have found in Catholic arguments, yours and others', a very high reasoning power. I'm not sure of my background here, but I assume this kind of reasoning could be called Aristotelian or Thomistic. I am tremendously impressed by the intellectual clarity, vigor, and system of Father Tanquerey in *The Spiritual Life*. Here is a genuine handbook of mystical and ascetical theology and practice. I very much appreciate your giving me a copy. I should have known from your frequent references to it and from your finding it indispensable that it would be a treasure. He has so much material that duplicates Evelyn Underhill's *Mysticism* that I am not going to send you the latter. You wouldn't find much new in it, and you would be annoyed at the juxtaposition of Protestant and Catholic mystics in her historical treatment. The two — Tanquerey and Underhill — were contemporaries, but neither mentions the other. This is another example of the tragic division between us that often keeps us from benefiting from each other's literature. I suppose the scholars on the top level are aware of the works on each side, but we lay people who are more or less at the mercy of our own religious periodicals for book reviews miss the works that are not published on our side. Thank you, too, for lending me St. Teresa's *The Interior Castle*. I have read much about her but nothing by her.

Tanquerey is a good example of the highly developed logical power I was mentioning. I am going to find his counsel quite valuable; but he is so much involved with a specifically Catholic framework that I should hesitate to mention his book to even devout Protestants as a reference. He deals in detail with each of the seven deadly sins and also with what some Protestant wag has called the "seven deadly virtues." I have been interested in the seven sins since sophomore English in college, where I encountered them in *Piers Plowman*. Tanquerey is wondrously thorough and very understanding of human nature. I can profit much from his advice. But I am used to thinking of sin, not sins. I am inclined toward Tillich's definition of sin as anything which separates a man from God, from his neighbor, or from his own best self. As for the virtues, I think it was good missionary strategy for the Church, in the first centuries of Christianity, to acknowledge the classical wisdom of placing a high value on prudence, justice, fortitude, and temperance and to add its own interpretations which went far beyond the classical understandings of these virtues. Of course I will not quarrel with the scriptural virtues of faith, hope, and charity which the Church added to make up the seven. It is profitable spiritually and morally to meditate on all these virtues; but it is foreign to me to dissect virtue so minutely. I am inclined to see grace, not virtue, as the final answer to sin, and with Tillich I find grace to be anything that unites me with God, with my neighbor, and with my own best self.

Catholic intellect seems to work best within a rigidly Catholic framework. I think we Protestants can learn something from you in clear, precise reasoning. Perhaps you can learn something from us in spontaneity and boldness of thought. One example of Catholic reasoning that has bothered me is the use of reason, not historical evidence, to support such a dogma as that of the Assumption of the Blessed Virgin Mary. I am sorry to keep returning to this dogma, but it is truly a stumbling block to Protestants. In *Our Sunday Visitor* for May 27, 1962, the Rev. Edward O'Connor has an article which follows a train of thought similar to your own in your third letter to me. Toward the end of his article he says, "But even someone who does not accept them can recognize that these doctrines originated, not as human fabrications, but as a result of meditation on the teachings of Holy Scripture." Well, I just can't accept meditation or reasonings as evidence for a historical fact. I believe that meditation and reason can be fruitful spiritually and intellectually but that they can lead one up mistaken paths.

Here, of course, we come again to the question of infallibility. Believing that your Church has it, you are naturally inclined to meditate and think within the framework given you. Not believing that God operates in such a way as to guarantee infallibility to any man or institution, we Protestants have learned to think and to meditate differently.

I feel that this letter is long enough already, and I am going to close without getting into the subject of birth control as I had hoped and planned. Maybe next time! The article you sent me on that subject, by the way, was weaker than your usual performance. I've not yet seen anything by a Roman Catholic about birth control that would be acceptable to anyone who didn't believe in the Church's infallibility.

But now I need to respond to a few things in your last letter. You very wisely suggest that I deal personally with the Jesuit I've been complaining to you about. I've known all along I should do that, and I'll try when I get a chance.

We two groups must get together on a common translation of the Bible acceptable to both of us, or we'll spend fruitless time and energy in argument over such a passage as you quote to me: "Unless you do penance you shall all likewise perish." I don't know what translation you are using, but it is not acceptable to St. Paul's original meaning in the Greek, to St. Jerome in the Vulgate, or to Ronald Knox. The Greek word unmistakably refers to a mental action (literally, "change your mind"), not to some prescribed exterior act of penance. Jerome translates it into a Latin phrase which means "have penitence." Knox simply says "repent."

I must get into St. Teresa before I try to discuss with you the various degrees of mystical experience. Just now, however, I want to send you two small books, both having to do with Protestant mysticism. I think you will agree with me that the authors have had a real experience of God. I had understood from your column that you did not consider such experiences available to Protestants. I'd like to get your reaction to Frank Laubach ("Letters by a Modern Mystic") and Thomas Kelly (*A Testament of Devotion*). Their experience is, of course, not in the Catholic framework, but it speaks to me with undeniable authenticity. The Kelly book gives a résumé of his life. Laubach is the pioneer and crusader for world literacy who originated the "each one teach one" strategy.

I am enjoying the *Southwest Catholic Registers*. Do you want them back? Next to your column, I like Msgr. Knott's best. He is exceptionally good on family life.

Love,

BETTY

✓ ✓ ✓ ✓ ✓

CARLSBAD, NEW MEXICO

September 27

Dear Betty,

I enjoyed sharing your reactions to the symposium on Space Age Christianity, agree with your contention that we need a more uniform numbering of Bible verses, and find your acknowledgment of the logic and high reasoning power of Catholic thinkers gratifying.

Did you, however, not detect a bit of inconsistency in your own arguments regarding the dogma of the Assumption? You say, "One example of Catholic reasoning that has bothered me is the use of reason, not historical evidence, to support such a dogma as that of the Assumption of the Blessed Virgin Mary." But the dogma of the Assumption is not founded on reason, though it is most reasonable; it is founded on a belief preserved in written and oral traditions of the Church from the very earliest times. You Protestants castigate us for our reliance on tradition, and when we attempt to point out that our traditions are not only backed up by extremely early written documents referring to them but that they are so logical that even one who does not accept tradition or the infallible teaching authority of the Church should be able to acknowledge that they are reasonable in a context of faith — then you chide us for using reason to support our dogmas. I don't specifically recall the

Our Sunday Visitor article you quoted but I assure you that I agree 100 percent with your own summary: "Meditation and reason can be fruitful spiritually and intellectually but can lead one up mistaken paths." That's exactly why Christ established a Church and endowed her with infallible teaching authority.

But to go back to the place of reason in religion, F. J. Sheed explores it pretty thoroughly in his *Theology and Sanity*, which I borrowed from the public library this summer and wished I could share with you. I bought a copy at the Madonna Shop in El Paso on my way to retreat last week and am forwarding it. He explains that while love of God is more important than knowledge of God, and while holiness is in the will and we are saved not by how much we know but by how much we love, knowledge of the truth matters enormously all the same. I think your own intellect is going to be stimulated and delighted by the boldness and clarity with which Mr. Sheed separates the chaff from the wheat. It took me almost two months to read the library copy; I had to renew it twice, not because it was dull but because it just isn't a book one should skim, so keep it as long as you like.

Have you realized that *grace* is another word that has a different meaning for Catholics than for Protestants? No Catholic could refer to grace as "anything that unites me with God, with my neighbor, and with my own best self." Grace may do any or all of these things, but that is not the essence of grace but a possible effect. I know you have a far better comprehension of the Protestant conception of grace than I had as a Protestant — to me it was simply a vague, pleasant-sounding word signifying God's favor. The Catholic meaning of grace as an actual help from the Holy Spirit enlightening our minds and strengthening our wills in the performance of supernatural acts and the avoidance of evil (see Tanquerey, paragraphs 124–128) was a revelation to me.

Catholics believe in two kinds of grace: actual grace, as above, and sanctifying grace (a better term is "supernatural life"). Let's see if I can explain the latter. There are different levels of being: for example, inanimate objects, plant life, animal life, human life, spirit life (angels), and the divine life of God Himself. Just as a rock can't acquire the life of a tree, nor a dog raise himself to the level of a man, so a man can't raise himself to the level of an angel, which is pure spirit. However, God has provided a means by which man can be born again on a different level, the supernatural level, and hence actually partake of His own divine nature, becoming a son of God and heir of heaven, without losing anything of his human nature. (The Second Person of the Blessed Trinity did this in reverse, being born again with a human nature without losing His divine nature.) This supernatural life is received in baptism and increased with every worthy reception of the sacraments instituted by Christ as channels of grace. It is not the exclusive property of Catholics but is given by God to all baptized Christians and also to those who through no fault of their own are not Christians but have an implicit desire to do what God wills; i.e., they love God and want to do whatever He wills; if they knew He willed that they be baptized, they would be.

This supernatural life, once acquired, is lost only through serious sin, which is in effect a turning of our backs on God and a deliberate rejection of His gifts. It is regainable in the sacrament of penance. It can also be restored outside the sacrament by an act of perfect contrition (i.e., heartfelt sorrow for our sin because it offended God, not merely because of fear of punishment or because it didn't bring the happiness we expected, etc.). Catholics must, however, have the intention of going to confession at the earliest opportunity. Thus the Church teaches that non-Catholics can and do have sanctifying grace, though they lack many of the opportunities for increasing it which are available to Catholics. "Actual grace" is also given to all, even to those not in the "state of grace" (not possessing sanctifying grace, either because they haven't been baptized or have lost it by sin). However, actual graces are not distributed equally to all, some receiving far more than others, though the Church teaches that all receive sufficient grace for salvation if they will cooperate fully. We can resist grace, because we have free will.

Your comments on Roman Catholics' use of statues being "not

necessarily idolatrous" and on our dulled "sensitivity to the dangers of graven images" amused me a good deal; I can't help feeling that you Protestants are making a great deal of to-do about nothing. I can see no idolatry or danger at all and it seems to me to take a great deal of wishful thinking (or of follow-the-leader *un*thinking) to make something dangerous or sinful out of the fact that we have statues and pictures and crucifixes in our churches and in our homes. The "images" are simply reminders and pious representations of those we honor and as such they can be immensely helpful in directing our thoughts and recalling our attention to God and the truths of our faith and reminding us of the good example and the present glory of those who went before us. We pray to the one they represent, not to the piece of marble or plaster or wood itself.

Were you ever a patient in a Catholic hospital? Didn't the crucifix on the wall remind you of Christ's sacrifice for you? Didn't it turn your thoughts toward God and move you to talk to Him in your heart in prayer whenever your eyes fell upon it? That is the purpose of our images. They are not idols to be worshiped in God's stead, as was the golden calf against which God and Moses fulminated, or the graven images to which the idolatrous neighboring tribes of the Old Testament Hebrews prayed. Didn't God Himself tell the Jews to fashion angels of gold to flank the Ark of the Covenant (Ex 25:18)?

I will concede that the emotional excesses of some people may tend to create false impressions among non-Catholics as regards certain "miraculous" statues or pictures of the Blessed Virgin or various saints, but the veneration or honor paid such images is still directed to God Himself, who has manifested His power and His mercy through these particular instruments. The veneration is always a result of extraordinary favors that could have come only from Him and that indicate His pleasure, as it were, in seeing the Mother of His Son honored under this title or that virtue. The glory of the saints is always only a reflection of God's infinitely greater glory — they but mirror His perfections and we look at them to see Him more clearly and adore Him whose grace working in them has made them what they are.

With regard to your objection to the words "do penance" in the quotation from Luke 13:5, I was quoting strictly from memory. On checking, I find that my Confraternity of Christian Doctrine translation of the Bible also says "repent," as does Knox. But I am sure that in my spiritual reading I have more frequently run across the wording as I quoted it (see Tanquerey, p. 341), and I imagine it is from the Douay version. Father Tanquerey's definition of penance ("a supernatural virtue, allied to justice, which inclines the sinner to detest his sin because it is an offense against God, and to form the firm resolve of avoiding sin in the future, and of atoning for it") could define repentance as easily. You might look up what Tanquerey has to say on penance and mortification, particularly paragraphs 746–750 and 767–770. I don't think I consulted *The Spiritual Life* when I wrote about penance in my last letter to you, but I believe what I wrote was consistent with his exposition and with the general teachings of the saints and doctors of the Church.

I was delighted with your remark about the weakness of the birth-control article (which, incidentally, was a reprint of a column written about two years ago). I had just discovered it in the current issue of *Immaculata* and clipped it and stuck it in mostly to see if it would get a rise out of you. You are right, it was weak; the arguments were mostly pragmatic (i.e., it's wrong because it doesn't work out as expected). But then, it wasn't intended as a dogmatic treatise on the subject. It was written in refutation of a reported resolution of some Baptists to the effect that since the financial burden placed on the parents by the birth of an unwanted child may result in the child's not being loved, birth control is both permissible and desirable. (And have you heard the old canard about *Catholics* preaching that the end justifies the means?) Actually, if you could see the difficulty I have writing the columns most weeks you would be amazed, as I am, that as many of them turn out as well as they do. Please criticize ruthlessly and don't hesitate to point out weak or fallacious arguments; you'll be a real friend.

As you will see from my column on the two little books you

sent me, I liked them both. However, besides the point mentioned in my column, that Dr. Laubach was pathetically unaware that the path he was traveling (trying to live each hour in continuous inner conversation with God and in perfect responsiveness to His will) was one that was so well known as to be practically traditional with Catholics, rather than the unique "experiment" he apparently assumed it to be, there was another thing that struck me profoundly. I quoted in an earlier letter to you Dale Francis' contention that it is not Catholics who place Mary too high but Protestants who place Christ too low; I was reminded of this every time Dr. Laubach mentioned Jesus in his letters to his father. He speaks of Jesus in terms a Catholic might use about St. Francis of Assisi or some other saint: i.e., "I saw a little of that marvelous pull that Jesus had as he walked along the road day after day 'God-intoxicated' and radiant with the endless communion of his soul with God." In none of his references to Christ does he seem to have the slightest comprehension of our Lord's *Divinity!* Christ is GOD, not a man with special supernatural graces. We are to follow Him, to imitate Him, yes; but we are to worship Him, too. And that's where Mary gets her dignity and why she is literally the Mother of God.

Lucile Hasley mentions the impression made on her by Caryll Houselander's *The Reed of God.* It's an exquisite little book; Father Klister sent it to me for Christmas a couple of years ago. I took it along on retreat last week — it's that kind of a book: you take it off in the garden under a tree, or into the church when nobody else is there, and you read just a little bit and without quite knowing when the transition occurs you are no longer reading but praying. It's more than a book; it's an experience. I'll send it if you're interested.

I'm glad you are enjoying the *Registers.* No, I don't want them back. I get my subscription copy on Thursday but Father gets a bundle which he puts in the church vestibule each Sunday for those who don't get their own in the mail, and there are always a few left over so I have no qualms about picking one up to send you. I had an unexpected windfall last week. A Canadian diocesan paper has been reprinting "Striving for Sanctity" from the *Wanderer*, with my permission, of course, and the editorship changed hands; the new editor informed me that he was also a "fan" and would go on clipping the column from the *Wanderer* to save me time, trouble, and postage but would henceforth pay me at their regular columnists' rate of $5 a week. A few days later the mailman brought a check for $25 for August!

I'm truly sorry about holding up our dialogue so long at this end all the time, but I really can't help it. I'm a fuzzy thinker and a snail's-pace writer — about one paragraph per hour is par.

Bye now. God bless you,

LORRAINE

✝ ✝ ✝ ✝ ✝

ETHETE, WYOMING

October 12

Dear Lorraine,

A typographical error in your column in the *Register* set me wryly chuckling and reflectively meditating. You wrote that Thomas Kelly knew and appreciated the *Imitation of Christ*. The typesetter changed it to *Limitation of Christ*. I get the impression that both Catholics and Protestants are guilty of the limitation of Christ in our popular thinking though not in our official theology. Now, I'm no longer interested in "winning points" from you in this conversation, which is not a debate. (And I was greatly touched and reassured by the fact that you have refrained from sending me the two pamphlets your fans have sent you toward my conversion. My original choice of the word "unreconstructable" to characterize my Protestantism was unfortunate, but I'm glad that you have learned to accept me as a true friend, unconvertible though I am. Maybe "hardtop" would be a suitable epithet for an unconvertible?)

In his book of Letters Laubach offended you with his references to Jesus. You felt that he put on our Lord the limitation of humanity without divinity. "He puts Christ where we put the saints. He does not worship Christ, he venerates Him," you expostulated in a note I found tucked into the little book of letters to Laubach's father. (You remarked in your last letter that you write about a paragraph per hour; I got into this paragraph and had to withdraw and read a 200-page book before I could continue. That took parts of two days.) I think it is helpful to realize that Laubach was writing these letters a generation ago (1930–1932), when "the Jesus of history" was of great interest in Protestant theology. Ministers trained in that generation were more likely than are ministers of today to speak of Jesus in a familiar way, as if they had just seen Him walking down the street. The Christology of today has grown deeper and one might even say more reverent as theologians have reawakened to the mystery of the Incarnation and tried anew to plumb its paradoxes.

Laubach may have erred in stressing too much the humanity of Jesus; are you Catholics, at least in your popular thinking, not prone too much to stress His divinity and ignore His humanity? You profess that he was "very God of very God," and so do we; but you seem not fully to accept the implications of His being a man. You grant that He is man, yes; but not a man, with human limitations. The Incarnation is a great mystery, and some of the finest Protestant minds are wrestling with it in our generation. Catholic theologians, too, are seeking to interpret the ancient creeds for modern minds. Sheed, and the others I have seen quoted, do not satisfy me that they have grasped the true humanity of Christ. They seem to be saying that God put on human flesh without accepting the limitations of a human mind.

One of the problems connected with how we think of Jesus Christ is the Liturgical Year which your Church and mine share. It's a good teaching device about the most significant events in the life of Christ, but it jumps so quickly from Epiphany to Lent that it may lead to the believer's neglect of our Lord's very important three years of public ministry, which reveal in many ways through the gospel accounts the humanity of the Son of God. It is through constant reading and rereading of the four Evangelists that many Protestants have discovered a Jesus whom they can call friend as well as Lord. True, Catholics have a devotion directed to the humanity of Christ in the Sacred Heart; but the representations of that romanticized anatomical heart on pictures and statues of Jesus amaze and alarm Protestants. We praise, bless, adore, glorify, and fully worship Jesus Christ. We acknowledge the mystery that He is both God and a man, and we have tried in various ways to elucidate this mystery. Wherever either side tends to oversimplify it, error rises up. You sensed the error in Laubach's view of Jesus; I mentioned several letters ago my dismay at the impression of Christ given in the book you lent me about appearances of the Virgin Mary — the impression that, if Mary weren't around to restrain His arm, He would be exercising terrible judgment on mankind.

Don't get me wrong. I too believe in Christ as Judge. But, without being able to explain it well and being unwilling to give even a digest of the 200 pages I've just read (it was "An Essay on Incarnation and Atonement" called *God Was in Christ* by D. M. Baillie — Scribner's, 1948), I must register with you my belief that the Jesus who is at the right hand of God in heaven is still our Mediator and Intercessor and is not joined in that place or in those functions by His mother. It seems to me that, although your official doctrine would not go so far, Catholics keep saying unofficially (and thus putting a tragic limitation on our Lord), "Well, Jesus is wonderful and all that, but He's *God;* He can't understand what it's like to be just human like us." Maybe this isn't what they are saying, but it is the message I get again and again from Catholic books and papers. So then they have to find somebody who will *really* understand the human condition, and they look to Mary.

Here we are again — or still — at Mary. I cannot accept your statement that "the dogma of the Assumption . . . is founded on historical belief preserved in the written and oral traditions of the Church from the very earliest times." The only written traditions from early times about the manner of her death are found in fantastic apocryphal writings which were early condemned by your Church. According to the *Encyclopaedia Britannica,* there is no evidence of the doctrine of Mary's perpetual virginity's having been taught within the pale of the Catholic Church of the first three centuries, and the doctrine of her absolute sinlessness was "originally quite unknown to Catholicism"; both Augustine and Anselm asserted that she was born in original sin. I honor Mary; I gladly call her Theotokos. If the fellows at Ephesus had meant to call her Mother of God, they could have easily done so: *Mater Theou* or *Theomater*. They chose the other title, and I'll stick with it: God-bearer.

About Tillich and me and grace: I probably did not do his thought justice when I tried to quote from a sermon I heard him preach 16 years ago. In a written volume of his sermons he discusses sin and grace without defining grace as I thought he had when I heard the sermon. He interprets sin as separation and grace as reunion and nowhere writes of "anything that separates" or "anything that unites." (The sermon is "You Are Accepted," in *The Shaking of the Foundations*, New York, Charles Scribner's Sons, 1948.) Anyway I don't think the Protestant conception of grace is so thoroughly thought out as the Catholic — although we are very fond of quoting from St. Paul: "For by grace are ye saved through faith; and that not of yourselves: it is the gift of God: Not of works, lest any man should boast" (Eph 2:8, 9, King James Version).

This quotation from Paul brings me to last Sunday's sermon in the little Roman Catholic church down the road, where I went for my annual visit. The priest (the same Jesuit I'm always complaining to you about), without mentioning the words Protestant or Reformation, referred to an error which arose in Christendom several hundred years ago, an erroneous position that it didn't matter what anybody did so long as he believed right. I suppose he must have been referring to Luther's insistence upon justification by faith, but of course he was oversimplifying that doctrine to the point that it made no sense and would be quite foreign to any Protestant, even to a Lutheran. It reminded me of the oversimplification I heard in my youth about Catholics, that they could commit any kind of sin they liked and then go and confess it to a priest and it would be all right. No, I haven't gotten any better acquainted with the Jesuit yet. He's not very approachable, and I'm not very bold.

In your helpful interpretation of the use of images by Catholics you ask whether I have ever been a patient in a Catholic hospital. Yes, I have. I don't remember a crucifix on the wall, but crucifixes do remind me of Christ's sacrifice for me. However, we Protestants strongly tend toward the cross, not the crucifix, as the central symbol of our faith — not because we lack artisans, but because we believe the story of the crucifixion is incomplete without the resurrection. A thoughtful Protestant theologian remarked some years ago that the Christ of the Roman Church in Latin America appeared to be either a helpless baby in arms or a dead man on a cross. (I was interested to see on Sunday that the Christ represented on the altar cross at the neighborhood Catholic church was Christ the King, Victorious. I didn't know this representation was used in your churches at all. Do you know whether it is a widespread use? I favor it, not because I would turn away from the sufferings of Christ, but because it acknowledges a completion to the story.)

The thing that I remember most about the Catholic hospital (besides a very young nun who looked like an angel and gave a glorious back rub) was its discouragement of mothers who wanted to nurse their babies. I've met similar discouragements in two other hospitals, but I reasoned that the Roman Catholics should be for natural law in baby-feeding since they were so strong for natural law in procreation. I've never succeeded in nursing any of our children for very long, and I don't know whether it's my physiology or my temperament that is deficient, but I'd like some expert advice and help and encouragement, not the attitude that women who want to breast-feed their babies are a nuisance and an unnecessary interruption to the hospital's schedule.

Now about birth control: we're for it, as I've said before. Although our Church has not taken an official stand on the subject, the bishops of the Anglican Communion meeting at Lambeth in 1958 accepted a report from their committee on "The Family in Contemporary Society" which I should like to quote at some length because I think it's good. I am quoting from

Section I, "Theology of Sexuality and the Family." This is not the whole report, or even a whole section of it.

THE PURPOSES OF MARRIAGE

To summarize, three purposes — three functions — are interwoven in human sexuality. Each of them is profoundly rooted in human experience and in God's revelation. The procreation of children, the fulfillment and completion of husband and wife in each other, and the establishment of a stable environment within which the deepest truths about human relationships can be expressed and communicated and children can grow up seeing and learning what mature life is really like — these are the great purposes which, in God's loving will, marriage and the family are created to serve.

RELATIONSHIP BETWEEN THE PURPOSES

It has been common, in Christian theology, to mention the procreative function first, as if to say that it is the ruling purpose. So it is, in the sense that no marriage would be according to God's will which (where procreation is possible) did not bear fruit in children. But it is clearly not true that all other duties and relationships in marriage must be subordinate to the procreative one. Neither the Bible nor human experience supports such a view. Where it has been held, the reason generally lay in a fear of the misuse of the sexual relationship or in a false sense that there is, in any sexual relationship, an intrinsic evil. Neither fear nor a false sense of what is "evil" is a helpful guide for humanity, in this or any other matter.

Responsible parenthood is both a more complex relationship and a far richer one than merely the reproduction of the species. Granted that the institution of the family is inescapably rooted in the biology of procreation and that this must always form part of the moral structure within which the decisions of husband and wife must lie, still the heart of family life — the heart of the marriage which is the cornerstone of the family — is the responsible freedom of the partners who make the marriage to begin with.

Indeed the whole enterprise of marriage and the establishment of a family is perhaps the most vivid expression we know of responsible human freedom under God. A man and a woman, free and competent to do so, agree before God and society to take each other as husband and wife, without reservation, for life. Any such adventure of free people carries with it both the privilege and the obligation of making the choices with which life confronts us. . . .

Techniques and devices for controlled conception now make it generally and easily possible to plan for parenthood at will. Thus the old, direct relationship between sexual intercourse and the procreation of children has been broken. The fear which has so often dominated sexual intercourse and the procreation of children has largely disappeared, and with it many of the accustomed disciplines of sexual conduct. And, in this new situation, there appear new problems for conscientious choice, and new possibilities for the marital relationship.

FAMILY PLANNING

The responsible procreation of children is a primary obligation. The questions, How many children? At what intervals? are matters on which no general counsel can be given. The choice must be made by parents together, in prayerful consideration of their resources, the society in which they live, and the problems they face.

It may be said, however, that responsible parenthood implies a watchful guard against selfishness and covetousness, and an equally thoughtful awareness of the world into which our children are to be born. Couples who postpone having children until certain financial goals are reached, or certain possessions gained, need to be vigilant lest they are putting their own comfort ahead of their duty. Similarly those who carelessly and improvidently bring children into the world trusting in an unknown future or a generous society to care for them, need to make a rigorous examination of their lack of concern for their children and for the society of which they are a part. . . .

But the procreation of children is not the only purpose of marriage. Husbands and wives owe to each other and to the depth and stability of their families the duty to express, in sexual intercourse, the love which they bear and mean to bear to each other. Sexual intercourse is not by any means the only language of earthly love, but it is, in its full and right use, the most intimate and the most revealing; it has the depth of communication signified by the Biblical word so often used for it, "knowledge"; it is a giving and receiving in the unity of two free spirits which is in itself good (within the marriage bond) and mediates good to those who share it. Therefore it is utterly wrong to urge that, unless children are specifically desired, sexual intercourse ought not to be engaged in except with the willing intention to procreate children.

It must be emphasized once again that family planning ought to be the result of thoughtful and prayerful Christian decision. Where it is, Christian husbands and wives need feel no hesitation in offering their decision humbly to God and following it with a clear conscience. The *means* of family planning are in large measure matters of clinical and aesthetic choice, subject to the requirement that they be admissible to the Christian conscience. Scientific studies can rightly help, and do, in assessing the effects and the usefulness of any particular means; and Christians have every right to use the gifts of science for proper ends.

Continence, self-control, and chastity have often been advocated on the basis of a view of life that identified the principle of evil with the "material" or "the flesh." Though we can no longer accept the dualism expressed in Puritanism and in the theology of St. Augustine, yet the Church holds as strongly as ever that continence, chastity, and self-control are a positive and creative element in Christian living. They are indeed an ingredient in an heroic and sacrificial response of man to the costly redeeming love of God. If Christian living were to be so influenced by current hedonism as to allow free rein to biological and sexual urges, it would lose the dimension of holiness and its power to challenge "the world."

In the man-woman relationship, not only before marriage but in it, chastity and continence are virtues of positive worth, sustained by the grace of God, for they release creative power into other channels. If the sexual relationship is to be truly an expression of partnership, the male has to recognize that his sexual urge may be the stronger and therefore he has more consciously to exercise self-control. Nothing that is said hereafter about the use of contraceptives in family planning takes away from the beauty and strength of abstinence mutually accepted.

The report goes on to discuss some of the means which are not acceptable to Christians, including "the wilful withholding of one partner from intercourse with the other. . . . (This, of course, does not refer to a mutual decision of husband and wife to agree to abstain from intercourse for a time as a particular and special offering to God.)"; "any means which interrupts or prevents the fulfilment of coitus" (the sin of Onan, a biblical fellow I'd never noticed until I started reading Catholic literature); induced abortion; and artificial insemination by any one other than the husband. It discusses sterilization at some length and concludes, "The choice of sterilization is a grave one, to be made only in deepest and most conscientious thought. . . ." This part of the report ends with the following paragraphs:

> The discussion of these specific questions has illustrated the complexity of the choices husbands and wives are daily called upon to make. They have a duty to bear children; they owe an equal duty to each other, of tender and completing love; and these two duties interpenetrate and lighten each other. Neither one should master the other, for then marriage is distorted and untrue. To keep them both in true balance is never easy, and the use of effective contraceptives, with its persistent invitation to sensuality and selfishness, is an added hazard.
>
> Yet to say this is to say no more than that no human relationship or dignity is easy to achieve. Marriage is a vocation as well as an estate of nature; it is an essay in responsible freedom; and we have no more right to expect it to be without its problems than we might expect good citizenship or personal integrity to be painless. Freedom is the condition of every human virtue and of every grace.
>
> Freedom is also the way towards the attainment of all that is excellent and true. And, perplexing though the choices in contemporary marriage are, it must also be said that the new freedom of sexuality in marriage in our time is also, and equally, a gate to a new depth and joy in personal relationships between husband and wife. At a time when so much in our culture tends to depersonalize life — to erode and dissolve the old, clear, outlines of human personality — Christians may well give thanks for the chance given us to establish, in marriage, a new level of intimate, loving interdependence between husband and wife and parents and children, freed from some of the old disciplines of fear.
>
> It must be said once more that this will not happen automatically. It will happen only when we deliberately choose it, and pay the cost of it in self-discipline, in courtesy towards one another within the marital tie, and in willingness to receive and give the fullest communication of love, physically as well as in every other way.*

* From *The Lambeth Conference 1958* (published in the U. S. A. by Seabury Press), pp. 142–150.

This is a terribly long quotation to throw at you, but I'd much rather throw the words of our bishops at you on this subject than try to say much the same things in my own words. I hope that, in spite of the fact that you must reject some of the things they say, you will grasp something of the depth of their Christian concern. I hope it's not being too crude to say that, if I were planning to take driving lessons, I'd much sooner trust myself to an experienced and skillful driver than to a man who had sworn never to set foot into a car. Most of the bishops who drew up this report are married men. I think they can speak more realistically and meaningfully about Christian marriage than all or any of the celibate Roman clergy can possibly do.

I'd better quit now. It's after midnight, and tomorrow is the day we clergy wives take off for three days in Laramie. Our Bishop (who was a member of the committee I've been quoting) suggests that the clergy baby-sit for these days! I am sorry to be keeping your St. Teresa so long. She isn't the sort of person one skims; and of course neither is Sheed. I'd like to see *The Reed of God* and also Lucile Hasley's *Reproachfully Yours.*

Somebody in Lander asked me one day how our dialogue was getting along and then asked, "Isn't she (you) — er — *extreme?*"

I answered, "Well, she's not fanatic, if that's what you mean."

"No; just — extreme. I mean, I have two sisters-in-law who are Catholic, and they don't *belong* to all those things, and all."

"But they aren't crackpot organizations; and she wants to be a saint — one of their kind of saints," I tried to defend you. I have a feeling that anybody who wants to be even a Christian these days has to be, in some ways and to a certain extent, "extreme"; don't you? My talk on Christian mysticism a couple of weeks ago was largely an exposition of the classic mystic way, using Evelyn Underhill's five divisions — awakening, purgation, illumination, dark night of the soul, and the unitive life, with illustrations from sources as varied as St. Teresa, St. John of the Cross, Harriet Beecher Stowe, and Florence Nightingale, with Laubach for good measure. I also indicated the mystical aspects of our corporate worship, inviting my listeners to deepen their own personal awareness of God and to learn to appreciate the contributions made by mystics, who tended to be quite practical persons. I hate to see mysticism relegated to a spooky fog when there is so much in it that is clear and normal and good. I feel that St. Teresa would have enjoyed and contributed to modern psychology if she had lived in these times. Still, she probably would be considered "extreme."

I'm acting like one of those guests who say good-bye and then stand around at the door for another half hour. It just means I hate to go. God bless you.

With love,

BETTY

✝ ✝ ✝ ✝ ✝

CARLSBAD, NEW MEXICO

October 28

Dear Betty (or *should I say* Hardtop?) —

You say in your last letter that Catholics are prone too much to stress Christ's divinity and ignore His humanity. I don't agree. While it may be that some Catholics do feel as you suggested ("Well, Jesus is wonderful and all that, but He's *God:* He can't understand what it's like to be just human like us") and look to Mary to bridge the gap, devotion to Mary is not meant by the Church to be an end in itself but a means to an end, leading men closer to Jesus. I think that because we are closer to Mary than you Protestants are, we actually appreciate His human nature (which He took from her, though He was God, not simply to satisfy man's debt to God by the Atonement but to make it easier for us to love Him) more than Protestants do. The very attention given to His infancy and to His passion and death which you decry in the Roman Catholic Church in Latin America are intended to emphasize the reality of His human nature, which you accuse us of minimizing. God became a helpless infant; He was nursed at Mary's breast, He grew up subject to Mary and Joseph, He did not disdain such social functions as wedding feasts. But neither Jesus nor Mary, I'm convinced, was ever ignorant of His simultaneous divine nature. She knew who His Father was. She sought His aid in saving their host at Cana embarrassment and He indulged her request with a miracle, even though His "hour" had not yet come.

Neither can I agree that the liturgical cycle neglects our Lord's years of public ministry: these are covered between Pentecost and the beginning of Advent, roughly half the year. It seems to me mystically fitting that Christmas and Easter should be celebrated in fairly close juxtaposition. At Christmas we adore the Child, on Good Friday we suffer with the Man, but it is the Resurrection that stamps the seal of verity on all that He taught and did during His earthly ministry. Thus, as far as the liturgical year is concerned, we begin with the prophecies and preparation for His coming, and the miraculous facts of Christ's birth, attested to by the shepherds and the Magi; after Epiphany we skip quickly over a few of the high spots in His story and come to His death and His Resurrection, which are the fulfillment of many more prophecies. Thus, in effect, the Church furnishes Christ's credentials (and her own — Pentecost) before presenting the main body of His doctrines.

Interestingly, I did not know that the cross without the corpus as used by Protestants is meant as a symbol of the *risen* Christ. Our use of the crucifix is meant to stir up our love for Jesus by reminding us always of the great love He had for us which manifested itself in such suffering and death in order that WE might be saved.

The representation of Christ the King is a fairly common one in Catholic churches, I should think. The last Sunday in October (today) is celebrated annually as the Feast of Christ the King, stressing, however, not so much His personal victory over death as His eternal Kingship over all individuals, families, classes, and nations. The Epistle is from Colossians 1:12–20 ("He has rescued us from the power of darkness and transferred us into the kingdom of his beloved Son") and the Gospel from John

18:33–37 ("Thou sayest it: I am a King . . . [but] my Kingdom is not of this world").

Don't you sometimes feel, Betty, that the differences between us (between Catholics and Protestants in general as well as between us personally), while important and undeniably *there*, are actually based mostly on misunderstandings and overemphasis and/or oversimplification of our respective beliefs? For instance, you mention that Protestants view Catholic devotion to the Sacred Heart of Jesus with amazement and alarm — but that is because they do not understand the theological soundness underlying all the popular sentimentality superimposed upon it. I'm going to send you a book by a Jesuit (!), Christian Pesch's *Our Best Friend,* which you will probably want only to skim; but at least do that, reading the points underlined (most of them marked six or eight years ago when I first read it, but a few marked this week when I went through it again in anticipation of sending it to you). You will see that it is, among other things, a refutation of the theory that Catholics think Jesus doesn't know what it is like to be "human like us." But as Father Pesch says, "The humanity of Christ is not our final aim and end. That is God alone. . . . The humanity of Christ is the way that leads to this end" (p. 17). Devotion to the Sacred Heart, as he explains clearly, is veneration for the person of our Savior, recognition of His love for men, a love symbolized by His physical heart which is "not the heart of Christ separated from His body, not the dead heart of Christ, but the living heart as it pulsates in Christ glorified." If you're interested subsequently in reading a life of St. Margaret Mary Alacoque, I'll send you *These Three Hearts,* which is also a biography of her confessor Blessed Claude de la Colombière and incidentally tells considerable about the training and spiritual formation of Jesuits, of which he was one.

On rechecking, I find that there is apparently no known written evidence of belief in the Assumption in the first three centuries. Daniel-Rops in *The Book of Mary* quotes Père Neubert: "'Some theologians have posited a local tradition about the Assumption, going back to the age of the Apostles and, little by little, spreading throughout the Church. They see in this the only way to explain the universal adherence to this truth. The existence of such a tradition is by no means to be discounted even though no trace of it be found in the older church writers. . . .'"* Who was it who said, "For those who won't believe, no proof is sufficient, for those who do, no proof is necessary"? The dogmas of Mary's perpetual virginity, her Immaculate Conception and her Assumption rest on a triple foundation: (1) they are altogether reasonable and logical developments of doctrines implicit in the Gospel itself; (2) the very absence of any evidence to the contrary (no church or city has ever claimed to have any relics of our Lady, though there are relics even of Mary's own mother, St. Anne) is a forceful indication that the belief in her Assumption dates back to the primitive Church; and (3) the fact that the infallible Church teaches that these doctrines are true. The last is sufficient for me.

It is possible, of course, for individual Catholics to "overdo" devotion to Mary in the sense that they put an excessive value on exterior practices such as novenas, rosaries, veneration of pictures or statues, etc., without any interior redirection of their lives. They remain in their sins, presumptuously confident that our Lady will save them despite the fact that they make no effort to stop offending her Son. As St. Louis de Montfort says, "How can we truly say that we love and honor our Blessed Lady when by our sins we are pitilessly piercing, wounding, crucifying and outraging Jesus Christ, her Son?"** Such presumption is, as I'm sure you understand by now, contrary to any teaching of the Church. True devotion to Mary is aimed at helping us achieve the intimate personal union with Jesus which is the fullness of the Christian life.

I am sorry that what you remember particularly about your stay in a Catholic hospital was its discouragement of nursing mothers. My own experience has been just the opposite. In fact, at St. Francis Hospital here they encourage nursing and will bring the baby to the mother whenever he's hungry even if they have to chase out visitors to do it, rather than give him a bottle or let

* *The Book of Mary* (New York: Hawthorn, 1960), p. 106.
** *True Devotion to Mary* (Bay Shore, N. Y., Montfort Publishers, 1958), No. 98.

him cry. If you or somebody you know wants really excellent advice and help on breast-feeding, write to La Leche League, 3332 Rose St., Franklin Park, Ill. This organization, started by a group of (Catholic) mothers who wanted to share the joy they themselves had found in "mothering through breast-feeding," offers a wonderfully helpful manual for mothers as well as a bi-monthly newsletter. Many hospitals make copies of the manual available to new mothers. I'll send you mine, along with a couple of articles describing their apostolate and a sample newsletter, just in case you've missed reading about them — maybe you'd like to help spread the good news.

It really seems that you have had more than your share of unfortunate experiences with Catholics — the unapproachable Jesuit, the unsympathetic hospital personnel, the priest who never reads anything written by women, etc. I am sorry. Your C. S. Lewis in *Mere Christianity* observes that we must not be surprised to find among Christians (this means Catholics too) some people who are still nasty. In fact, he suggests, there is even a reason why nasty people might be expected to turn to Christ in greater numbers than "nice" ones. The "nice people" are in danger of being so satisfied with themselves and so self-sufficient that they may fail to realize their need for God. The nasty ones, on the other hand, if they make any attempt at goodness at all, learn quickly that they need help: they are the "poor," the lost sheep Christ came especially to find. "That was what people objected to about Christ during his life on earth: He seemed to attract 'such awful people.'"

Incidentally, while I'm quoting C. S. Lewis, let me share this wonderful passage from the same book with you:

> . . . Already the new men [i.e., transformed not by Evolution but by Baptism, from creatures of God to sons of God — L. J.] are dotted here and there all over the earth. Some, as I have admitted, are still hardly recognizable: but others can be recognized. Every now and then one meets them. Their very voices and faces are different from ours; stronger, quieter, happier, more radiant. They begin where most of us leave off. They are, I say, recognizable; but you must know what to look for. They will not be very like the idea of "religious

> people" which you have formed from your general reading. They do not draw attention to themselves. You tend to think that you are being kind to them when they are really being kind to you. They love you more than other men do, but they need you less. (We must get over wanting to be needed: in some goodish people, specially women, that is the hardest of all temptations to resist.) They will usually seem to have a lot of time: you will wonder where it comes from. When you have recognized one of them, you will recognize the next one much more easily. And I strongly suspect (but how should I know?) that they recognize one another immediately and infallibly, across every barrier of color, sex, class, age, and even of creeds. In that way, to become holy is rather like joining a secret society. To put it at its very lowest, it must be great *fun.**

The five-page quote from your Bishops' report was interesting, though I'm afraid they don't speak with enough authority or enough consistency to be very convincing. (In 1920, here's what they said: "We utter an emphatic warning against the use of unnatural means of avoidance of conception, together with the grave dangers — physical, moral and religious — thereby incurred." In their official statement at that Lambeth Conference they upheld "the primary purpose for which marriage exists — namely, the continuation of the race through the gift and heritage of children" and pointed out "the paramount importance in married life of deliberate and thoughtful self-control.")

The Catholic Church does not oppose family limitation when circumstances make it advisable. What she opposes is anything that deliberately destroys the physical integrity of the marriage act. Abstinence from union, with mutual consent and for a morally good reason, is not sinful and can be highly virtuous, involving as it does the exercise of self-control, continence, chastity, etc. But performing the act with the deliberate intention of frustrating its natural end by chemical, material, or physical means is intrinsically evil. The Church says so, and I assent. You said earlier that you had never read anything Catholic on the subject that was convincing to one who does not accept the infallibility of the Church. For me, that's enough.

* *Mere Christianity* (New York: Macmillan, 1955), pp. 172–173.

With reference to your comparison about taking driving lessons from experienced drivers, I could suggest that those who have no personal ax to grind are apt to look at things more objectively: "concerned with God's claim" rather than "the world's claim" (cf. 1 Cor. 7:32–33). However, the veracity of the teaching rests neither upon the experience nor the objectivity of the human teachers but upon the inerrancy of the Holy Spirit who speaks through His Church.

Thanks for defending me against the charge of being a fanatic, though I must admit I've been called that before and it doesn't upset me. I agree with you that anybody who wants to be a Christian today has to be "extreme." At a Third Order Communion breakfast recently the priest speaker called Tertiaries the "core" of the parish and then made a neat play on words by characterizing us as the "spiritual Peace Corps" of the parish. We are followers of St. Francis, who was certainly an extremist—but was anyone ever more extreme than our Lord Himself? He preached no doctrine of compromise and concession: "If thy right hand offend thee, cut it off! . . . He who loves father or mother more than Me is not worthy of Me. . . . Sell all thou hast and give to the poor and come, follow Me! . . . Care not that the world hates you . . ." and much more.

I'd better get this in the mail—I started typing it on the Feast of Christ the King and now it's the Feast of All Saints. I'm asking them all to pray for you.

With much love,

LORRAINE

✝ ✝ ✝ ✝ ✝

ETHETE, WYOMING

November 12

Dear Lorraine,

I was praying for you, too, on All Saints' Day, not to the saints but to God for one of his saints. (Have you discovered the Saints' section in our hymnal? I especially like Ralph Vaughan Williams' setting for No. 126, "For All the Saints.") Then I was interested to find a description of St. Alphonsus Rodriguez (feast day, October 30) in a recent copy of the *Southwest Catholic Register*. A friend, comparing housewifery with Alphonsus' doorkeeping as an occupation, years ago sent me Gerard Manley Hopkins' Petrarchan sonnet "In Honour of St. Alphonsus Rodriguez, Lay Brother of the Society of Jesus" (those Jesuits again!). Are you acquainted with it? It is fitting for a housewife-saint:

Honour is flashed off exploit, so we say;
And those strokes once that gashed flesh or galled shield
Should tongue that time now, trumpet now that field,
And, on the fighter, forge his glorious day.
On Christ they do and on the martyr may;
But be the war within, the brand we wield
Unseen, the heroic breast not outward-steeled,
Earth hears no hurtle then from fiercest fray.

* * *

Yet God (That hews mountain and continent,
Earth, all, out; who, with trickling increment,
Veins violets and tall trees makes more and more)
Could crowd career with conquest while there went
Those years and years by of world without event
That in Majorca Alfonso watched the door.*

Hopkins' poetry is hard to "dig" sometimes, but there's apt to be gold, as well as "freshness deep down things." Another kind of freshness delights me in Lucile Hasley's books, two of which you have lent me. I have made a note of some of the Catholic authors she mentions — Alfred Wilson, Chesterton, Péguy, Walter Farrell, Gerald Vann, and Caryll Houselander, whose *The Reed of God* I am enjoying. You have, a bit apologetically, sent me a couple of books which were meant just for Catholics and which seem to be characteristic of a genre. (I mean the one about the appearances of Mary and the recent mailing on Devotion to the Sacred Heart.) The style of these, as you guessed, does not appeal to me; but both have served your purposes in sending them to me to skim. I think I'll skip *These Three Hearts*,

* Gerard Manley Hopkins, *The Poems of Gerard Manley Hopkins* (London: Oxford University Press). Used by permission.

thank you; between my other reading and St. Teresa, I haven't had time to begin to do justice to Sheed's *Theology and Sanity*, which has meant so much to you that I want to get into it. (Your wholehearted recommendation of a book is something I dare not ignore. It reminds me of the occasions, once in a very long while, when Ware comes home and says, "I met somebody today that I think you'd like." He's always right about such people.)

Yes, I think many of the differences between us are based on misunderstanding and overemphasis or oversimplification of each other's beliefs. I find that, whenever I attempt to state a belief or an emphasis of Catholics as I see it (one that I don't like), you don't agree at all with the way I state it. I'll admit I started this conversation with you partly out of curiosity: "How can an intelligent person believe all that?" Now that you have welcomed me into your heart, I still acknowledge that you are intelligent; I perceive that you do believe "all that" in a very full and intelligent way; and I appreciate both you and Roman Catholicism in a way that I didn't dream was possible. The wall is still there, but its shape is different from what I expected. I still don't look for any sudden miracle of reunion, but with Catholics like you and Hans Küng around, I see a basis for hope. Some of the liturgical changes being suggested at the Vatican Council, if put into practice, could make your Church more comprehensible to the rest of us. And of course "the rest of us," in all our diversity, have a long, long way to go before we shall be ready for reunion, either with you or with one another.

I appreciate your sending me La Leche League Manual and the other material about and from this remarkable group. I'd read about the newsletter in a bibliography of maternity education publications; and last month at Clergy Wives' Conference one of the wives expressed enthusiasm about the League. I have ordered a copy of the Manual to lend to the mothers whom I introduce to childbirth information. (Childbirth education has the force of a vocation for me — along with three or four other vocations. I hope to learn much more about it and to spend more time on it when our children are older.)

No, our bishops don't speak with the kind of authority you

want about birth control or anything else. Our Church government is largely republican, with laymen represented along with priests and bishops. I don't think you and I will get anywhere in discussing contraception, but I know it is a subject of much guilty concern to ordinary Catholics. I have sat in an obstetrician's waiting room listening to three Roman Catholic mothers-to-be, two of whom admitted using mechanical contraception between babies. "I confessed it to my priest and he told me not to do it any more," one of them said, "but I know I will." She didn't mention her husband's attitude, but I have wondered what the emotional atmosphere must be in mixed-faith marriages in which the Catholic partner favors abstention for the sake of family planning and the Protestant partner won't go along. The ideal answer, of course, is for Catholics to marry Catholics and for Protestants to marry Protestants; but often that isn't the way it works.

I believe it is our Christian duty as parents to use our God-given intellect to decide how many children we can bear and raise to the glory of God. There are times when I make a frightful mess of it with our four; I'd hate to have the responsibility of any more. Some women may find their primary vocation in bringing up larger numbers of children. My God-given intellect tells me I am better at other things and counsels me to do the best I can with the children we have and then to serve God in other ways.

I liked the quotation from C. S. Lewis. I don't think I've read *Mere Christianity*. I've been wanting to get his book of commentary on the Psalms. *Perelandra* and *Out of the Silent Planet* are excursions of his into science fiction (spiritualized) which you might enjoy. I get the impression you have a pretty good public library available. Ours is 17 miles away and usually doesn't have anything I am looking for.

I've been wanting to ask you how it is with you and schools. Four of yours are in school, aren't they? Senior high, junior high, and two in grade school? Do they all go to parochial schools? How much does it cost? Do you feel that the religious training they get is more valuable in some age periods than in others? I understand that canon law requires Catholics to send their children to parochial schools if they are available. I don't have any particular questions beyond those I've asked, but I'd like to have your opinions and comments on schooling.

My own experience with Church-related schooling was at college. Agnes Scott is not owned or controlled by any Church, but it was founded by and is largely governed by Presbyterians, and its present president is a Presbyterian minister. (When I was there, the president was a dedicated and influential Presbyterian lawyer, but on his retirement the trustees ruled that future presidents must be ministers. I think that decision was a mistake.) I shall always be grateful for those four years in an intensely intellectual community where Christian thought, life, and worship were actively encouraged. Not all the faculty members were Presbyterians, but all were engaged as both scholars and Christians. Those who were less fully committed Christians than others refrained from airing their disbeliefs. Nobody was slapped down for heresy or unbelief, but the prevailing tone was constructively religious. My family had very little money and I had to work much of my way to and through college (I stayed out a year after high school to get a financial start); I could have gone at much less expense to the state university, but I much preferred the Christian college. It never entered my father's head to complain about having to share in the support of the state university while sending me to another kind of college. Likewise if we should decide to send any of our children to a Church-related prep school, we would accept the extra cost and still consider it our duty to support the local public high school.

I read somewhere recently that most religious education for Catholics (including priests' education) consists of memorizing a great deal of material. Is that right?

This seems to be shaping up as a busy week. Tomorrow Ware, David, and I join the other Episcopal ministers of this deanery (coincident with the county) and their wives and preschoolers for Communion, luncheon, and a program on the theology of the ecumenical movement. Tomorrow evening we go to the airport (31 miles away) to pick up a visiting expert, a priest-sociologist from Maryland who is serving this year as a consultant for the Church's social welfare work among Indians. He will stay with us two or three nights and will be joined on Thursday by two more priests who have some responsibility for the work here. They may or may not stay here Thursday night; I'll invite them if the visiting expert leaves a bed free by then. On Friday evening the two other priests and a lot of other people and Ware and I plan to go to a little town an hour away from here for the ordination of a young priest. Ware has invited another priest and his wife from a farther-away town to spend that night with us. There's going to be some fast sheet-changing (and sheet-washing) around here. Saturday is relatively free, Sunday is always very full, and Monday night I am supposed to talk to some Methodist women in Riverton about our dialogue. I don't know how much (for how many meals) I'll be feeding the visiting experts, but I have to be prepared to feed them every meal with lots of coffee in between. One time I found myself alone in the kitchen with a priest-expert I'd just met. He sat on a kitchen stool and we talked while I went about preparing dinner in my awkward, haphazard way. He was a good conversationalist and I enjoyed the visit. It wasn't until some time later that I learn that one of his favorite interests was time-motion study! Oh, well. These fellows have charity along with their expertise.

Love,

Betty

✝ ✝ ✝ ✝ ✝

J. M. J.

Carlsbad, New Mexico

December 30

Dear Betty,

Christmas is over — at least, the feast is over, though the spiritual joy and liturgical celebration linger on. I cherish your gift dearly. *The Hound of Heaven* is one of the few Catholic poems I am reasonably familiar with and I am happy to have it in a volume all to itself; the woodcuts are striking. But it is the giver who makes the gift precious.

Thank you. And thank you, too, for quoting the Hopkins sonnet in your last letter. I must admit I've read very little poetry since college days — lack of exposure, lack of incentive, no one to share it with — and I'm grateful to you for opening new doors and reopening old ones. Isn't it a strange twist this dialogue has taken — you, the Protestant, introducing me to Catholic poetry? I found Péguy's *God Speaks* delightful, especially these lines from "Sleep":

> I don't like the man who doesn't sleep, says God.
>
> * * *
>
> . . . they tell me that there are men
> Who work well and sleep badly.
> Who don't sleep. What a lack of confidence in me.
>
> * * *
>
> I pity them . . .
> Poor children, they conduct their business
> with wisdom during the day.
> But, when evening comes, they can't make up their
> minds,
> They can't be resigned to trust my wisdom for the
> space of one night
> With the conduct . . . of their business.
> As if I wasn't capable, if you please, of looking
> after it a little.
> Of watching over it.
> Of governing and conducting, and all that kind of
> stuff.
> I have a great deal more business to look after,
> poor people, I govern creation, maybe that is
> more difficult.
> You might perhaps, and no harm done, leave your
> business in my hands, O wise men . . .
> And the next morning you might find it not too
> badly damaged perhaps. . . .*

Father spoke in his sermon this morning (December 30) of

---

this being the time to take inventory, and there is a thanksgiving service at the church tomorrow evening to end the year with gratitude for all the blessings God has bestowed on us during the course of it. I think the 1962 gift from God I value most highly is our friendship, which is surely from Him and for His glory, and which has brought other blessings in its wake — an appreciation of Protestant mysticism, for one; a richer understanding and interest in the Council, thanks to your sending me Fr. Küng's book; the awakening to the "freshness deep down" of poetry.

Another great blessing of this past year, to me, is the music God has put under my fingers and in my heart. When I started the piano lessons it was with the intention of getting ahead of the kids so I could teach them; I would have considered it a luxury we couldn't afford, an extravagant self-indulgence, otherwise. But that didn't work out, partly because I'm just no good at teaching — I couldn't make it interesting enough to keep them wanting to learn, though my own lessons with Mr. B. are fascinating highlights of the week; partly because I was never here evenings to enforce their practicing and Joe resents any noise except what comes out of the TV when he's home. So my kids aren't learning any music, but I'm soaking it up like a sponge and don't think I'll ever get saturated. When I started I told Mr. B. I just wanted to learn enough to be able to play hymns and songs; the older boys can't carry a tune but Mary loves to sing and has a nice voice and I think the younger ones will sing, with encouragement and accompaniment. He told me I wouldn't be content to stop there, and he's right. I want to play Chopin and Bach and Beethoven and Brahms, and I don't want to stop taking lessons, because I know it's only the necessity of practicing for a lesson and having definite progressive assignments and criticism and correction that keep one advancing.

But I have had many scruples about it. Is it a side road, a distraction, that, while good in itself, comes between me and attainment of the highest good — union with God? Is it God's will that I spend so much time and effort training fingers which, at best, have a relatively short time left to bring pleasurable sounds from a man-made contraption of wood and wire? Mr. B. is a believer in reincarnation and feels that in a subsequent lifetime we can start in more or less where we left off — that's how he explains musical geniuses and child prodigies — but I doubt if there will be pianos in heaven. . . . As the Voice asked St. Francis, "Which is it better to serve, the servant or the Master?" I seem to find it impossible to get away for even one hour of meditation and silent prayer before the Blessed Sacrament; but I manage to get away for a music lesson every week, that lasts an hour to an hour and a half, even if I have to pay a baby-sitter. I don't practice any formal daily meditation, but I practice the piano for at least an hour right after breakfast most mornings, letting everything else go until later, because I've found if I start out with the other things the day will slip by without my getting any practicing in.

Oh, Betty, I have such ups and downs — mentally, spiritually, emotionally. One day about a week before Christmas I sent you a mental S.O.S.: things are rough here, hold me up lots. Did you get the message through telepathy? (I also called my favorite priest that day and told him I was about to take off for the moon and did he want to give me his blessing before I left. He said he could suggest a better place to go — to the Blessed Sacrament in the tabernacle. I didn't manage to get to either place that day, but the next day things were better.)

Believe me, I know what you mean when you say your intellect tells you you're better at other things than raising large numbers of children. Me too. At least, I couldn't be worse! I have a sister who really is a saint, wise and good and full of patience and charity. She doesn't read (or very little, at any rate, outside the Bible); she prays and works and loves. Her kids don't quarrel and talk back to her and pick on each other, as ours do, and her husband is apparently an ideal husband and father. She must have some cross, but I don't know what it is and I doubt if anyone would ever find out from her. They have nine children of their own and one foster daughter and still want a dozen. In principle I'm still in favor of large families; but coming down to personal cases, I have no desire for any more children, though I will not commit sin to prevent it. Of course that stand causes conflicts in mixed marriages, as you observed. But "he who loves father or mother more than me is not worthy of me" — etc. Some things you can't compromise on and stay friends with God. And the one who would ask you to betray your conscience: how long could you count on *him*, do you think, before he would in turn betray you? "All things betray thee, who betrayest Me." I'll stick with God and the Church, thanks, and God help the Catholics who don't.

I meant to discuss religious education and the school support issue but time is running short and I want to get this into the mail before another week goes by so I think I'll just answer your questions briefly this time. Three of ours are in Catholic schools: Mary and Tony in the elementary school next to the church, Mike in the junior high (5th through 8th grades) a mile and a half away. There is no Catholic high school in Carlsbad. Tuition is $5 a month for the first child, $10 for two or more in the same family. The junior high was built about five years ago on a large tract of land with room for a football field and baseball diamonds and also another church if the town grows enough to make it desirable to divide the parish; it has a large multipurpose gymnasium with a kitchen, and I think eight classrooms, and is designed to permit the addition of another wing of classrooms later. Children are turned away from the elementary school because of lack of room and there is a waiting list, as in most parishes. I think there is a great deal of value in giving our children a religion-oriented education, intended to make religion a natural, normal part of all life, not something to be thought about or given lip service on Sunday and ignored the rest of the week. In Tony's first reader, for instance, along with the "Go up, David. Come down, Ann," there are things like this: "Jesus, help me. Help me find Ann. Jesus can help Mother. Jesus can help Ann. Jesus can help you." The Masons and POAU find this scandalous, a form of brainwashing. I think it's fine. Very little of the actual facts they learn may be remembered but the atmosphere of faith that surrounds the child will surely have its impact on the subconscious level.

I would like to send the older ones to a Catholic high school; there is a Jesuit boys' high in El Paso I would give a great deal to be able to send Mike to next year. One weakness in our local parochial school system is the absence of male teachers. I would be very strongly in favor of segregated (by sex) education, at least in the junior high and senior high grades, with men teaching the boys.

Your question about religious education for Catholics consisting of memorizing a great deal of material sounds like one of those half-truths or loaded questions. Our children do memorize their catechism (Who made you? God made me. Why did God make you? God made me to know Him, love Him, and serve Him in this world and be happy with Him forever in the next. . . . On a higher level: What do we mean when we say that God is the Supreme Being? When we say that God is the Supreme Being we mean that He is above all creatures, the self-existing and infinitely perfect Spirit. What is a spirit? A spirit is a being that has understanding and free will, but no body, and will never die. What do we mean when we say that God is self-existing? We mean that He does not owe His existence to any other being. And so on.) The emphasis is on understanding what the answer means rather than parroting the answer word for word, but they are required to answer the questions and the easiest way to do it accurately is by memorizing it. They also memorize occasional poems, their multiplication tables, and the like. In Sunday School, we used to get prizes for memorizing Bible quotations, the names of the books of the Bible in order (I can still rattle 'em off, King James version). Essentially, I can't see a whole lot of difference.

There is a catechetical movement in the U. S. which is constantly striving to present religious truths in a more engaging and compelling way, stressing the need for awareness of the scriptural background underlying Catholic dogma and a deeper understanding and participation in liturgical worship, as well as a vital relating of the truths of faith to daily life. I'm all for this, but I'm for memory work, too.

I understand the current trend in public schools is to de-emphasize memorizing. I took a course at the Community College here in Creative Writing a couple of winters ago and the teacher was a young man just barely out of college whose knowledge of writing was strictly from textbooks. He spent one entire evening reading poetry aloud to us and said he never had his pupils memorize anything as it "spoiled their enjoyment of poetry." I disagreed strongly, as did another middle-aged woman there, who vied with me after class reciting poems we had memorized years ago, which meant far more to us now than when we committed them to memory.

I *must* stop; Joe will be home any minute and I'm due at work in less than an hour. I did want to say I don't know how you manage to feed and entertain all the visiting clergy and celebrities. I don't think I could do it, though I presume with the need comes the grace, since that's part of your state in life.

God love you.

LORRAINE

ETHETE, WYOMING
January 7

Dear Lorraine,

I'd planned to write you a real letter tonight but first have to conquer resistance to the new postal rates. (Actually, I had to deliver a message 14 miles over slick roads and found the time and energy used up that way.) Loved your long letter. I'll be awhile answering it. Ware and I are off to Denver tomorrow for a couple of days' rest and fun. We have to give a talk on Indian work in Cheyenne Friday, then home Saturday. Next week big shots again.

Thank you for the bookmarks and the leaflet on mental prayer. I'm embroiled in ½ dozen books on Indians, marriage, etc. Our county (Deanery) Episc. Clergy group met today and discussed Küng. We plan to continue same study next month.

I think I got your S.O.S. the week before Christmas. Tried to answer. My own static sometimes blocks the line.

Love,

Betty

✓ ✓ ✓ ✓ ✓

Ethete, Wyoming

January 25

Dear Lorraine,

I've just realized it's *weeks* since I wrote you and since your letter came. I wanted to answer it soon and am looking for a block of time. Maybe I'll have to settle for moments here and there. Denver was quiet but fun. I bought a stack of paperback Catholic books and will list them so you can indicate which ones you'd like to borrow. *The Love Letters of Phyllis McGinley* is one. Do you know her poems? It's been almost a year since you and I "met."

I'm sending *The Reed of God* — beautiful! Also a sample book of prayers for children for you to keep. I'll explain in letter.

Love,

Betty

✓ ✓ ✓ ✓ ✓

Ethete, Wyoming

January 27

Dear Lorraine,

I've let the time get away from me since receiving your last letter. Your letter arrived January 7, in the middle of a meeting here of clergy and wives of this deanery. (The program consisted of a discussion of Küng's first two chapters.) The next day Ware and I took off for Denver on our annual (sometimes it works out to be biennial) trip together. I hadn't particularly felt a need to get away this time, but the first night in the hotel room I woke up three times listening to the silence and suddenly realizing that I had no responsibilities, either to our children — safe with a baby-sitter — or to anyone who might be outside in the night. (We are often awakened by the doorbell or the telephone at weird hours in the night and predawn; emergency does not sleep on an Indian reservation.) When the telephone finally did ring, at 9:15 a.m., we were both sound asleep but willing to wake up. The caller was a retired college professor of mine whom we always see when we go to Denver.

We saw a few movies, visited my professor, bought some books and some powdered milk in bulk, and rested all we wanted. I had a new hairdo. On Friday we drove to Cheyenne, where we talked about our church work to 25 women who had braved the bitterly cold weather (20 degrees below zero with a biting wind). Next day, after a delightful visit with a fellow alumna of Agnes Scott College and her family, we drove home. The following week we entertained two visiting clergymen in connection with our mission's work. Last week was shot to pieces by a one-day trip to Casper (150 miles away) for a district (diocesan) committee meeting.

My husband and I were both very much interested in your description of what music has meant to you in the past year. He nodded his head firmly and said, "It's healthy." He himself sometimes sits down to the piano and spends a whole evening playing Beethoven, Mozart, Haydn, and others.

I've been trying to find, in all my literature on mysticism, some exposition of the Way of Affirmation. I can't find it, but I know there is such a term to set over against the Way of Negation in the believer's quest for union with God. Now, your pals St. Teresa and the other cloistered women whose lives you have been reading obviously chose the Way of Negation, which is a valid way. May it not be part of your task to explore the Way of

Affirmation? You acknowledge that God has put the music under your fingers and into your heart. You admit it is good in itself. You may have 30 years or more left to bring pleasurable sounds from that man-made contraption, the piano. (You may, of course, have less than a day. Isn't it funny how the secular press has reacted to your dear Pope's assertions that he's ready to go any time? Some of the papers have made headlines out of this very simple Christian attitude; some of them have read into it dire premonitions.) Whether we have 30 years or a day, I believe we have to say Yes to life while it lasts, and Yes to our condition in life. A saint-to-be with a husband, seven kids, and a daughter-in-law has to approach life differently from a saint-to-be with a cell and an ordered daily communal life. "God saw everything that he had made, and behold, it was very good." Who are we to contradict God and say that what He has made is evil? We are always bewailing the evil use to which men put God's good things; but who is to pioneer in enjoying and using the good gifts of God? The Psalmist bids us praise God upon the strings; a piano will do, I think. I don't share your piano teacher's confidence in reincarnation; Incarnation itself is enough to convince me that God sees our human, earthbound life as worth living. To the full.

Here I'm going to take issue with you on an otherwise acceptable list of rules for happiness in one of your recent columns. You say, "DON'T — read secular magazines, books, or papers any more than you can help. Their materialistic, pragmatic, secularistic views will insidiously undermine your supernatural faith, hope, and peace of mind." I know what you're saying, and I know a person can get bogged down in secular reading to the exclusion of spiritual reading. (My! Our life is simplified here in Wyoming by the absence of bulky twice-daily papers.) But I think a Christian can get a great deal out of so-called secular reading. (My life isn't compartmentalized into sacred and secular. God is at the center, and everything I find in life is related to God.) Of course I believe in selective reading; I skim newspapers and magazines very rapidly and thus read a tremendous amount of material in a short time, mentally discarding most of it. But I would rather take a first-rate "secular" magazine, like the *New Yorker* or the *Saturday Review*, than a fourth-rate "religious" magazine. Almost every issue of the two magazines I've mentioned feeds my spirit. The articles may not have a distinctly "religious" slant, but they are perceptive, thorough, and informational in such a way that I can grow through them. Similarly some of the so-called "religious" movies are far less radically religious than some of the works of drama written by Tennessee Williams, William Inge, and Arthur Miller. When a work of literature or drama unveils the needs of a fellow human being in a way that makes me understand and more fully love my neighbors, I call it religious. That is, I bring my own religious understandings to it and incorporate its truths into my religious insight. Almost all Jesus' teaching illustrations come from the "secular" world, in which I believe He took a hearty interest. The Christian religion *is* materialistic and contains much in it that is pragmatic. You go to Mass every day. This is a very materialistic thing to do, and it is a very materialistic thing that is done there. Couldn't the priest just as well be spiritual about the whole thing and forgo the Bread and the Wine? Couldn't you be more spiritual and just stay home and think spiritual thoughts? No, he couldn't. No, you couldn't. Jesus suggests some quite pragmatic tests to separate sheep from goats (St. Matthew, Chapter 25). I don't see anything in there about how many saints' lives the sheep had read or the goats hadn't read. "By their fruits ye shall know them," was another pragmatic test of his.

One reason I'm being so hard on you about laying hold on life is that these thoughts have come to me largely in the years since I have been part of a Church that calls itself Catholic as well as Protestant. As another Presbyterian-turned-Episcopalian said to me, "The Episcopal Church taught me to have fun." I wonder whether the Roman Catholic Church hasn't been teaching you to have fun too, while you've been ignoring its teaching and clinging to your Presbyterian Puritanism? I'm not sorry to have been a Puritan; but I'm glad not to have to be one any more. Ware can't believe that I went through college, with honor, without ever studying on Sunday. (I note that Roman Catholic interpretations of the Sabbath commandment exempt studying from the category of work that isn't to be performed on Sunday; but I still like for our girls to have their homework done before Sunday, so they can know the true restfulness of one free day.) I'm much less strict than I used to be about the day, but I still treat it as very special. You mention having "scruples" about your piano playing. Scruples is a word I didn't know, in the Roman Catholic sense, until I started reading your literature. I think it's a wonderful concept — a scruple as "an unreasonable fear and anxiety that one's actions are sinful when they are not, or mortally sinful when they are only venially sinful," according to your *Catholic Almanac*, which is now mine. I had always thought of scruples as something good, or at least not ungood, to have. Your Church is sane in warning against them. (Of course, to me, sin is sin; I don't go in for this venial and mortal business.) It seems to me to be saying: relax. Love God, and play that piano!

In all our time lapses I've not had a chance to tell you about our latest episode with the local Jesuit. Before Christmas he came to see Ware about a baptismal record. We asked him to stay for coffee and had a most pleasant chat! I didn't confront him with any of the accusations about him that I've been flinging at you; I didn't think we were well enough acquainted. Later he sent us a Christmas card with a friendly note of appreciation for the baptismal information. I hope we'll see him again, often enough so we can begin to talk frankly. We are on very friendly terms with the Jesuit who frequently swims in the hot springs pool when we do; but in a swimming pool the talk doesn't get serious. Being quite nearsighted, I probably wouldn't recognize him if I saw him on the street.

I didn't mean to insult your Church's educational methods when I asked about memorizing. I think it was in an article on the Vatican Council that I read the statement that much of a priest's education consists in memorizing material. (The author was speculating that creative thinking might be rare among the bishops.) Did you ever memorize the *Shorter Catechism?* I did, and I've found it a handy peg on which to hang my later thoughts. I agree with you on the value of memorizing poetry, multiplication tables, and other things too. Being mostly ignorant about parochial schools, I wasn't asking intelligent questions. I agree with you on the value of having God-related textbooks. We try, in our religious education, to help people relate everything in life to God. (By the way, I'd like to borrow a copy of the *Baltimore Catechism* if you can spare it.)

I've kept your *Theology and Sanity* much too long but am now getting into it and will try to get it back to you soon. This week I sent you (along with *The Reed of God*) a little book of interpretation of the Our Father and the Hail Mary, published as an Anglican edition of an obviously Catholic book. Copies of this and a similar-type coloring book arrived as free samples in the mail last week, and I think you will have more use for the book than we will. It is an example of some Anglican thought and teaching. As you must have realized before now, our own Church has a long way to go before it is in unity with itself. I am sure that many of the opinions I have expressed in our dialogue would be repugnant to some Anglicans; that's why I have styled myself a Protestant rather than an Episcopalian.

One Roman Catholic practice that I like, and that I haven't mentioned to you, is the practice of "offering things up" to God. I have been in the habit of offering up my joy and gratitude; but the idea of consciously offering up my troubles and my sufferings had not become real to me until I kept finding it in your writings and the writings of other Catholics. Thank you!

Yes, I think I got your mental S.O.S. before Christmas. I know what it is to have ups and downs — mentally, spiritually, emotionally, and physically. I feel that I have come to understand myself a great deal better in the past 10 years or so, and consequently the downs have been less deep. Sometimes when we have spoken on our work to a church group, the women will come up to me and ask, "What can we do for you?" I suppose it would be practical to ask them for money, but there is something we need much more, and I answer, "Pray for us and for our people and for our work." What a simple thing to do! So simple that I'm afraid it isn't done nearly enough. I pray for you; it is the best thing I can do for you; or you for me.

With love always,

BETTY

⸗ ⸗ ⸗ ⸗ ⸗

[Between January 27 and August 4, the letters between Lorraine and Betty did not stop. On the contrary, they became more frequent and less formal, filled with details about the doings of their 11 children, concerned about each other's activities, still loaded with references to books and ideas. They discussed Mother Seton, Solange Hertz, different kinds of love (*eros* and *agape*), what promises Roman Catholics and Episcopalians make in the marriage services, Lent, God's providence and man's responsibility for his own choices. What had started out as a chips-on-shoulders intellectual argument between religious antagonists had developed into an ever-deepening friendship between sisters in Christ.

[During these months a series of luncheon meetings began between Roman Catholic priests and the Episcopal priests (with their wives) in Fremont County, Wyoming. Subject for discussion was Küng's book *The Council, Reform and Reunion* (N. Y., Sheed & Ward, 1961). Through these meetings Betty became much better acquainted with the Jesuit priest working on the Indian Reservation and found him "likable, keenly intelligent, with a good sense of humor." She avoided complaining to him as she had complained to Lorraine about his activities, but the general feeling was that relations between the two churches had never been better on the Reservation.

[The two typewriter-pals kept seeking ways to meet each other in person, and they managed to get together in Wyoming for parts of five days during the first week in August. After having known each other intimately for so long, it seemed strange to have to get superficially acquainted. Together they prayed, silently, in Our Father's House, the Episcopal chapel at Ethete;

together they attended Mass at St. Stephen's, the Roman Catholic mission on the Reservation; together they went to an Episcopal funeral at St. James' Church in Riverton. They hiked together beside Jenny Lake in the Tetons, watched Indians dancing in costume at the Arapaho Powwow, and on a three-hour trip to Casper sang Protestant hymns in harmony with one another. On the bus on the way to Wyoming Lorraine had written this letter:]

✝ ✝ ✝ ✝ ✝

J. M. J.

SOMEWHERE BETWEEN
CARLSBAD AND DENVER

August 4

Dear Betty,

I am writing this on the bus, on my way up to visit you. I don't think I have ever, in all my life, looked forward to anything with such a serene joy. I haven't the slightest qualms or doubts that we won't get along or won't be able to converse — commune is really the word I mean — with each other without pretense or wariness. I'm not even afraid of Ware. I want him to play both the piano and the organ for me!

What do you think about winding up our Dialogue with a pair of letters recapitulating and reaffirming our respective religious beliefs and attitudes?

To start with mine (just because this was my idea and you are welcome to the last word): I'm open-minded on almost any subject in the world, except one. I was open to conviction on it also, until February, 1951, when through reading and prayer I became utterly, absolutely, unfalteringly convinced in my mind and in my heart and in my soul that the Catholic Church, under the successors of St. Peter, the Bishops of Rome, is the living Church, founded and established by Christ to transmit His truths and His grace to men till the end of time. I believe that only in union with Rome is there full union with the Holy Spirit whom Christ promised to send to His followers to keep them in truth. I believe that all Christians who, individually or aggregately, are not in full communion with Rome, partaking of the same seven Sacraments, acknowledging as true all the dogmas declared by Rome as *de fide*, are literally *separated brethren*, brothers in Christ who have left home and who may save their souls and even do much good where they are, but who can only find the fullness of spiritual truth and joy attainable by souls in this life by returning home to the One Fold under the One Shepherd. When they return — again either individually or aggregately — they may (and I'm sure they will) bring much of value with them from wherever they have been, enriching the Church with insights and values and practices acquired during their separation. I believe that day will come — not in our lifetime, probably, but before the end of this world. I am unutterably, overwhelmingly grateful to God for the grace of my own personal conversion: it is a gift I treasure so highly I would give my life rather than lose it; a gift I pray — with fervor but with full submission to God's inscrutable will — that He will bestow in His own good time to *all* who have not received it.

Now — will you analyze and tell me as clearly and logically as possible, why (aside from not having received the grace of the Gift of Faith, which is the reason *I* assign to it) you are still not drawn to the Roman Catholic Church, after all your Catholic reading and thinking of the past year?

This is not meant to try to start any controversy or put you on the defensive — *you know that*. I love you deeply and respect your beliefs and anticipate feeling far more at ease and in communion with you spiritually during our week together than I would feel in many Catholic homes, because there will be no (or relatively little, and that as likely to be on my side as yours) padding of secularism and materialism to deflect us and to prevent our making contact.

See you soon! I'll give this to you while I'm there and you can answer at your convenience.

With love,

LORRAINE

✝ ✝ ✝ ✝ ✝

ETHETE, WYOMING

August 15

Dear Lorraine,

"Conversion is not my aim," I wrote in my first letter to you; but I'm sure an honest look into my motives would have revealed at least a small hope that you would "see the light" — the Protestant light. Now you want to know why I am still not drawn to the Roman Catholic Church, after all my Catholic reading and thinking of the past year.

One ready answer is that, along with all that Catholic reading and thinking, I have been spurred to do an equivalent amount of Protestant reading, the best of which I could not share with you. All along, I have been able to be more truly catholic in my reading and in my thinking because I do not accept the authority of the Roman Catholic Church.

Why do I not accept that authority? Because, through reading, prayer, and thought, I have become convinced that God does not operate in the way the Roman Catholic Church asserts that He does. I see the history of the Judaeo-Christian faith as showing God at work through peoples, nations, individuals, and institutions, but never guaranteeing any people, nation, individual, or institution to be the infallible instrument of His grace. From moment to moment, from eon to eon, He uses the personal and institutional instruments which are, at that moment and in that eon, responsive to His will. I love and serve my own Church but consider it (though it has endured for centuries and probably will endure for centuries longer) a temporary institution which will eventually become part of a greater, unified Church of believers in the Lord Jesus Christ. I believe the Holy Spirit works in and through history, individuals, and groups, not especially through any guaranteed institution. I believe He even bypasses the Church and the Churches to accomplish His will when He finds it necessary.

I further believe that He has worked His will richly in you through the Roman Catholic Church. Through you, I now appreciate and love your Church in a way I never dreamed possible; but at the same time I reject its absolute claims more firmly now that I understand them better.

I started this discussion, a long time ago, with questions about freedom. In one of your informal letters to me you wrote the following:

"I agree with you that freedom is important. But freedom doesn't mean just doing what one pleases. Only God is perfectly free, and He Himself is, in a sense, voluntarily limited in carrying out His designs by the free will He has chosen to give men, which enables them to refuse to obey or serve Him.

"I feel that I am making the most intelligent use of my freedom in voluntarily submitting to the authority of the Church Christ established to lead men to God and to distribute God's graces to men. I entered the Church of my own free will (though it was God's grace and not any worthiness of my own that led me to it). I remain in it of my own free will. I obey the laws and directions of the Church voluntarily because I believe obedience to the Church is, ultimately, obedience to God. I could read anything you can read (provided it's in English!) but I prefer to read only books which will strengthen my faith and help me to grow in wisdom and understanding and virtue.

"Keep your freedom, if you choose; as for me, I choose what I think is the higher freedom: voluntary servitude to God on His terms, not mine."

Beloved, the freedom I keep yammering about is not so far from the voluntary servitude you have chosen. I too believe that God's service is perfect freedom. I just don't accept the Roman Catholic

Church as my guide in how best to serve God. I believe that part of the way God works is to give us all — persons and institutions — the freedom to do or not to do His will. I believe that this freedom applies to the Catholic Church as to any other, and that the history of the Catholic Church shows her exercising her freedom both gloriously to do His will and ingloriously to thwart His will. I could outline some more arguments; but they would be taken from books you don't want to read. I feel an interest now in preserving and protecting your faith, not in subverting it.

In all our conversations I realize that I haven't conveyed to you any true Protestant sense of the Church. Roman Catholic literature (and some Anglican literature about Protestant groups) tries to give the idea that Protestant Churches are just clubs, or sermon societies. I have not found them so. I have found the Church, what I believe to be the true Church, as I have worshiped with Baptists, Moravians, Lutherans, Methodists, Nazarenes, Presbyterians, and others, as well as with Episcopalians. Corporate worship means a great deal to me: I do not think a person can be a Christian alone. My finding the Church among all these various groups does not mean that I am religiously indifferent. I have my preferences in form of worship and statement of belief. But I believe the Church of Jesus Christ is to be found in every fellowship of believers in Him, and I have recognized His Holy Spirit operating in many diverse groups. While fresh air is blowing through the Roman Catholic Church these days, the Spirit of God seems to be working also in Protestantism to heal the divisions among us. Numerous denominations have already formed organic unions with one another, and others are entering into conversations with one another to explore the possibilities of union.

Although Protestants are taking steps toward coming closer together, disagreements still rage among various viewpoints, including the approach to Scripture. I don't know whether you are acquainted with the term "Biblical criticism." It refers to scientific investigation of the Biblical texts to discover their origin, history, and original form. In effect it has meant seeking to treat the Bible like any other literary work. Fundamentalists and literalists have screamed at the idea of such an approach; men like Robert McAfee Brown, co-author with Gustave Weigel of *An American Dialogue* and author of *The Spirit of Protestantism* (N. Y., Oxford University Press, 1961), would say that any new knowledge about the Bible is to be sought and welcomed as part of God's truth.

Brown, and many other Protestant scholars, belong to the tradition that would eschew "proof-texts." Realizing that we have moved into a completely different world since the sixteenth century, they acknowledge that we can no longer accept the Reformers' view of the Bible. Brown distinguishes between the Word of God (Jesus Christ) and the words of Scripture, and finds, in Luther's description of Scripture as "the manger in which Christ lies," a way to "retain a Protestant emphasis on the centrality of Scripture, and still do justice to the fact that we live in the twentieth century."

Living in the twentieth century means, among other considerations, that both you and I, both Roman Catholics and Protestants, must face the fact that a large part of our world doesn't give a damn about Protestantism or Catholicism. Christianity today seems irrelevant to a great many intelligent persons, meaningless to nationsful of people. You and I, to whom Jesus Christ means everything, are much closer to one another than either of us can be to those to whom He means nothing. This is the way Abba Dorotheus, an Eastern Orthodox mystic, expressed a similar thought thirteen centuries ago:

> Imagine a circle and in the middle of it a center; and from this center forthgoing radii-rays. The farther these radii go from the center, the more divergent and remote from one another they become; conversely, the nearer they approach to the center, the more they come together among themselves. Now suppose that this circle is the world: the very middle of it, God; and the straight lines (radii) going from the center to the circumference, or from the circumference to the center, are the paths of the life of men. And in this case also, to the extent that the saints approach the middle of the circle, desiring to approach God, do they, by so doing, come nearer to God and to one another . . . Reason similarly with regard to

> their withdrawing — when they withdraw from God, they withdraw also from one another, and by so much as they withdraw from one another do they withdraw from God. Such is the attribute of love; to the extent that we are distant from God and do not love Him, each of us is far from his neighbour also. If we love God, then to the extent that we approach to Him through love of Him, do we unite in love with our neighbours; and the closer our union with them, the closer is our union with God also.*

Our disagreement, yours and mine, your Church's and mine, is deep and basic. But at the same time our faith in One Lord, together with our love for one another in Christ, is deep and basic. Whether the world knows it or not, the world belongs to God. I believe it is God's will that our Christian witness to the world be united. At this point in time the obstacles to unity seem almost insurmountable; but if unity is God's will, and if we are all seeking to know and to do God's will, I believe that unity will come — perhaps not in the ways we look for it, perhaps not on the timetable we would set for it, but in God's way, in God's time.

Let us go on from here!

With love,

BETTY

P.S. Thank you for saying I could have the last word, but I think it would be better if you had it. You haven't had much of an inning lately.

B.

✝ ✝ ✝ ✝ ✝

CARLSBAD, NEW MEXICO

October 22

Dear Betty,

I wonder if the people who will read these letters will be able to see how very much (surprisingly to both of us, I think) we've

* From *The Choice Is Always Ours*, ed. by Dorothy B. Phillips (New York: Harper & Row), pp. 412–413.

grown since we started? Each of us felt we could teach the other a good bit: did we have any idea that we ourselves would profit so enormously?

I know I didn't. I answered your first letter happily, welcoming the chance to tell you all about the Catholic Church and possibly make a convert of you. I felt, as most Catholics do, that the definitive word had already been spoken on most theological matters: we had the truth, the whole truth, and nothing but the truth, and in one book or another I could find the answer to any question you might ask. However, as a Catholic editor wrote recently, the fact of the matter seems to be that we don't have the truth, the Truth has us; and it is the awesome responsibility we have to the truth that should make us tremble, lest we be obscuring it where we should be making it a shining beacon for the world.

Cardinal Cushing wrote a pastoral letter to the clergy and faithful of his Boston Archdiocese last April that brings this out clearly. The believing Christian, he says, sees the world in the hands of its Creator, who has revealed Himself through His Son and pointed out the path, planned in His wisdom, for man's happiness. To accept this revelation is not a blind submission nor an abdication of reason; it is rather the intelligent acceptance of what would otherwise be beyond our human knowing. Far from closing off our view of life and reality, it opens up new vistas. It is in this context, Cardinal Cushing asserts, that the authority of the Church, as guardian of this divine message, must be seen in its true proportions. "Neither cramping the human spirit nor narrowing the areas of knowledge and intelligence, its first function is to open gates which lead into new ways, to guide souls to an understanding of the mysteries that God Himself has revealed."

There is an obligation on the part of authority toward this revealed truth and its integrity in time, he declares. The bishops, as lawful successors to the Apostles, have the obligation to preserve essential Christian doctrine without change, but at the same time to encourage public opinion and private judgment "within those wide boundaries where its contribution will be helpful to a fuller understanding and a broader application of the Christian message." It is never easy to maintain the balance between authority and freedom, he points out, and history has given us many examples of excesses in one direction or the other. But our knowledge of the truths of Faith is not merely a matter of intellectual exchange, not just the transmission of fixed ideas from mind to mind. "*The mature Christian is expected to use his own gifts to clarify his understanding of Church doctrine, and the human mind can have no higher function than to explore to its capacity the mysteries of God.*" (Italics mine.)

I am so glad the Council is seriously considering the role of the laity in the Church. Cardinal Cushing is manifestly one member of the hierarchy who feels the lay Christian has not only a right but an obligation to make himself heard, within his sphere of competence; to bring his insights and talents to the treasury of the Church and to expect that "his opinions will be treated with respect and his influence accepted when it is constructive and helpful."

In fact, I am so glad there is a Council! Pope John opened the window and let a fresh breeze through the Church, all right; few of us realized at the time what a blessing it would be and how badly we needed it. Various writers and speakers in the past year or so have compared the Church to a house filled with bric-a-brac and souvenirs, cluttered with mementos and treasures accumulated in the course of the centuries and held onto through sentimental reasons or habit or inertia long after the need for them has passed. The members of the family, most of them, simply take the clutter for granted, scarcely seeing it; but the children who have left home look at it with less sympathetic eyes. "Why don't you get rid of that old thing?" they ask. "It's useless and takes up so much space!" "Oh, we couldn't!" is the shocked reply. "Why, that's been in the family for centuries! Home wouldn't seem the same without it."

I, for one, while believing firmly and with all my heart that the Catholic Church is holy, indefectible, the Bride of Christ, the Mystical Body of Christ, the Holy Mother of all Christians everywhere, agree with those who think it's time for a big housecleaning, with lots of fresh air sweeping through the house and lots of the stuff that clutters up the rooms cleared away.

The Latin of the Mass is a good example — perhaps the most obvious one. When you asked me, back in the spring of 1962, how I felt about the vernacular in the Mass, I was for keeping the principal part of the Mass in Latin, though I did think the fore-Mass, the instructional portion, would be better in the vernacular. I used my own experience in attending Mass at San Jose Church as an example of the at-homeness a Catholic feels wherever the *Dominus vobiscum* is said. Well, I'll have to eat those words. San Jose has recently initiated a Dialogue Mass in Spanish. The priest still says the Mass in Latin, of course, but silently, while a lay leader reads aloud the psalms and prayers and Scripture selections in Spanish, and the people respond antiphonally and sing Spanish hymns in the appropriate places. It's wonderful! The joke (on me) is that I found it *more*, rather than less, intelligible and inspirational than the conventional Latin Mass I defended so stanchly earlier.

You should hear those people (and there were scores more worshipers present than on weekdays a year or two ago) sing those Spanish hymns! The second time I went, I was singing right along with them: *Bendito, bendito, / Bendito sea Dios; los Angeles cantan / y alaban a Dios. Creo Jesus mio / que estais en el Altar, / oculto en la Hostia / te vengo a adorar. Por amor al hombre / moristes en la Cruz / y al ara desciendes / por nuestra salud. Bendito, bendito. . . .* I'll send you one of the *Misa Dialogada* booklets that Father Gonzalo had printed. Even if you don't know Spanish (I had one year in college, which isn't too much help) you can tell what they're saying if you're familiar with the missal. I was making all the responses with them too, but not very loudly because I didn't know how to pronounce all the words. Of course I had to follow the Epistle and Gospel in my own missal.

Under our new pastor we've started a similar program at the 8 a.m. Sunday Mass at St. Edward's, which is the one I almost invariably attend: with congregational hymn singing and a layman reading and interpreting the Proper of the Mass during the service. (Hans Küng, by the way, calls the translator-reader a temporary solution to the problem of liturgical participation in the vernacular, which will disappear "as soon as the priest himself is permitted to speak, as in the early centuries, directly to the people in a language intelligible to all of them.")

I'm sending his *The Council in Action* (New York: Sheed & Ward, 1963), which I've been reading with much interest. One thing he brings out, that I had not realized until I read this book, is that the changes being debated in the Council today are to a great extent fulfillment of "valid Protestant demands for reform." For example:

1. The revaluation of Scripture in Catholic dogma, exegesis, preaching, and private reading;
2. Development of the liturgy into a genuine people's community worship, with return to the vernacular and congregational singing;
3. Sense of the universal priesthood of believers;
4. Increased adaptation of the Church to the needs of the nations and the existing cultures in mission areas;
5. Depoliticizing of the Papacy and decentralization of administrative power, with renewed emphasis on the authority and relative autonomy of the bishops;
6. Growing appreciation of tolerance and the individual conscience;
7. The reassessment of the role of Tradition;
8. Giving the cup to the laity, at least on certain special occasions, and a closer approximation of the liturgy of the Mass to the pattern of the Last Supper without detracting from its essential character as a sacrifice.

You'll be especially interested in his chapter on the missions. He says the ecumenical spirit is more lagging in the missions than elsewhere, and gives as part of the reason the competition between Catholic and Protestant missions in the same territory and the old-fashioned apologetic slant of much religious literature, which attacks the teachings of the "adversaries" rather than showing love of them as separated fellow Christians. I would assume that the Wind River Reservation in Wyoming has had its share of this unecumenical spirit, but that the climate has changed a lot in the last year. Right?

A Catholic editor recently suggested a connection between the absence of a "viable liturgical sense" in this country and the fact that in too many parishes the only chance the people have to sing English hymns is at such devotions as novenas to Our Lady of Perpetual Help. My own feeling is that there is a connection, all right, but not in the direction he implied (i.e., that it is an exaggerated, unhealthy devotion to Mary and the saints that is responsible for the dormant liturgical awareness). I would say that people have an instinctive, built-in need to sing together and pray aloud in unison and that it is because they haven't had any opportunity to do this in the Latin-rite Catholic Mass for centuries that they flock to devotional services where this need finds a legitimate, if inferior, outlet. I find myself eagerly anticipating the liturgical reforms which will flow from the actions of the Council.

I was interested in your discussion a few weeks back on the Protestant approach to the Bible as exemplified in Dr. Robert McAfee Brown's *The Spirit of Protestantism.* At that time I didn't really know enough to comment intelligently on it, but a very enlightening book on biblical criticism, Luis Alonso Schökel's *Understanding Biblical Research* (New York: Herder & Herder, 1963) has helped me greatly. I was afraid it would be dull and difficult to understand but was pleasantly surprised. The author, a Spanish Jesuit, explains in extremely readable popular style, full of concrete examples, just what biblical criticism is: the search for the most authentic text, uncorrupted by copyists' or translators' errors, additions, or changes (only the original is inspired, not the subsequent translations); and the endeavor to understand the intention and meaning of the inspired writer and why he expressed his inspired thoughts in that particular form and style—which involves also, of course, a study of the age and culture in which he lived. Father Alonso Schökel's exposition of the historical background of biblical criticism is fascinating. The early Fathers of the Church, he shows, were primarily concerned with the mystical and allegorical meanings of Scripture. At the time of the Protestant Reformation the Reformers used the Bible as a polemic weapon, and its interpretation became so controversial that the Catholic Church felt it necessary to restrict its unsupervised reading by the laity, though still encouraging scholarly study. Then in the Age of Rationalism some Protestants went in for critical research and scientific methods in biblical study but rejected *a priori* all that was supernatural or miraculous, endeavoring to explain everything in the Bible in terms of psychological or natural phenomena. To the Rationalists, Scripture, particularly the Old Testament, was simply a religious literary document of unique historical significance but of no practical personal application.

In reaction, the Catholic Church became ultraconservative. She looked on Rationalism as a serious threat, even a diabolical one: to deny the supernatural is to deny the possibility and necessity of salvation. As a result, nineteenth-century Catholic biblical scholarship was overshadowed by fear: of possible errors, of the contagious influence of Rationalism and Modernism, of compromising the integrity of revelation and the value of the sacred books. Pope Leo XIII's encyclical *Providentissimus Deus* in 1893 for the encouragement and direction of biblical studies, and the foundation by St. Pius X in 1909 of the Pontifical Biblical Institute for scriptural research and professorial training were steps in the right direction.

But it is really just within the past thirty years or so, Father Alonso Schökel shows, that Catholics and Protestants have begun to see the value in each other's work and have been working together instead of against each other. Thanks largely to Karl Barth, he states, Rationalism is a thing of the past, and though Protestant scholars may disagree about the explanations or avoid them entirely, many of them now accept the divine inspiration of Scripture and the reality of God's supernatural intervention in the affairs of men at various times in history. However, he says the general public is still about fifty years behind in its attitude, looking with suspicion upon even the words *biblical criticism* in the belief that they imply "criticizing" the Holy Book; and scandalized by the statements of scholars that some of the Old Testament stories they have accepted literally are actually fables or allegories conveying religious truths.

You quoted Dr. Brown on the distinction between the Word

of God (Jesus Christ) and the words of Scripture ("the manger in which Christ lies" — Luther's phrase). A German Jesuit, Gustav Closen, is quoted by Father Alonso Schökel in this book as making a different sort of analogy (which appeals to me more): he notes that the thoughts of God are by nature divine and purely spiritual, but when He puts down His thoughts in writing for men they must be clothed in the garb of human thought. As Jesus took His flesh and blood from Mary and must have closely resembled her physically, the spiritual child engendered by the inspired prophet or evangelist bears a close resemblance to the human author. The qualities of the human writer can be deduced from the qualities of his inspired book. Thus the spiritual child is son to both the inspired author and the word of God, he says, in much the same fashion as Mary's child was His Mother's Son, but also the Word of God.

I feel sure there will be a great reunion of Christendom some day. Only God knows how it will take place. In the meantime, you and I, at least, have the joy of knowing we have taken our own personal steps toward a deeper understanding and love in Christ. Many of the walls between us are down, never to be reraised. Others will, I hope, fall in time.

I can think of no better way of closing my last letter in our book than with the words of the hymn we sang together in the car on the way from Ethete to Casper last August, while Ware napped in the back seat and David sat happily between us:

Blest be the tie that binds
Our hearts in Christian love;
The fellowship of kindred minds
Is like to that above.

Before our Father's throne
We pour our ardent prayers;
Our fears, our hopes, our aims are one,
Our comforts and our cares.

We share our mutual woes,
Our mutual burdens bear;
And often for each other flows
The sympathizing tear.

When we asunder part,
It gives us inward pain;
But we shall still be joined in heart,
And hope to meet again.

God bless you, Betty, always!
LORRAINE